FINANCIAL INDEPENDANCE

A 21st Century Approach

DAVID HOLMAN

Table of Contents

Title Page
Copyright
Front Matter
Table of Contents
Introduction
Understanding Financial Independence
Defining Financial Independence
Benefits of Achieving Financial Independence
Setting Financial Goals
Short-Term Goals
Long-Term Goals
Budgeting and Saving
Effective Budgeting Techniques
Strategies for Saving Money
Income Streams
Traditional Employment Income
Passive Income Sources
Real Estate Investments
Dividend Stocks
Online Businesses
Investments
Basics of Investing
Types of Investments
Stocks
Bonds
Mutual Funds
ETFs
The Power of Compound Interest
Understanding Compound Interest
Maximizing Compound Interest
Retirement Accounts
Introduction to 401k
Benefits of IRA
Roth vs Traditional IRA
The Infinite Banking Concept
What is Infinite Banking?
Implementing Infinite Banking
Real Estate Investments
Introduction to Real Estate Investing
Types of Real Estate Investments
Tax Strategies for Wealth Generation
Understanding Tax Brackets
Tax-Efficient Investing

- Protecting Your Wealth
- Importance of Insurance
- Types of Insurance
- Creating a Financial Independence Plan
- Steps to Create Your Plan
- Adjusting Your Plan Over Time
- Conclusion
- Appendix
- Financial Independence Resources
- Recommended Reading

Financial Independence
A 21st Century Approach

by
David Holman

Copyright 2024 David Holman. All rights reserved.

No part of this book may be reproduced in any form or by any electronic or mechanical means including information storage and retrieval systems, without permission in writing from the author. The only exception is by a reviewer, who may quote short excerpts in a review.

Although the author and publisher have made every effort to ensure that the information in this book was correct at press time, the author and publisher do not assume and hereby disclaim any liability to any party for any loss, damage, or disruption caused by errors or omissions, whether such errors or omissions result from negligence, accident, or any other cause.

This publication is designed to provide accurate and authoritative information with regard to the subject matter covered. It is sold with the understanding that the publisher is not engaged in rendering professional services. If legal advice or other expert assistance is required, the services of a competent professional should be sought.

The fact that an organization or website is referred to in this work as a citation and/or a potential source of further information does not mean that the author or the publisher endorses the information the organization or website may provide or recommendations it may make.

Please remember that Internet websites listed in this work may have changed or disappeared between when this work was written and when it is read.

Financial Independence: A 21st Century Approach

Contents

Introduction

Chapter 1: Understanding Financial Independence
- Defining Financial Independence
- Benefits of Achieving Financial Independence

Chapter 2: Setting Financial Goals
- Short-Term Goals
- Long-Term Goals

Chapter 3: Budgeting and Saving
- Effective Budgeting Techniques
- Strategies for Saving Money

Chapter 4: Income Streams
- Traditional Employment Income
- Passive Income Sources

Chapter 5: Investments
- Basics of Investing
- Types of Investments

Chapter 6: The Power of Compound Interest
- Understanding Compound Interest
- Maximizing Compound Interest

Chapter 7: Retirement Accounts
- Introduction to 401k
- Benefits of IRA
- Roth vs Traditional IRA

Chapter 8: The Infinite Banking Concept
- What is Infinite Banking?
- Implementing Infinite Banking

Chapter 9: Real Estate Investments
- Introduction to Real Estate Investing
- Types of Real Estate Investments

Chapter 10: Tax Strategies for Wealth Generation
- Understanding Tax Brackets
- Tax-Efficient Investing

Chapter 11: Protecting Your Wealth
- Importance of Insurance
- Types of Insurance

Chapter 12: Creating a Financial Independence Plan
- Steps to Create Your Plan
- Adjusting Your Plan Over Time

Conclusion

Appendix A: Appendix
- Financial Independence Resources
- Recommended Reading

Introduction

Welcome to a journey that many dream of, but few embark on with a clear and practical roadmap: achieving financial independence and generating lasting wealth. You're here because you aspire to live a life where money isn't a constant source of stress, where financial flexibility allows you to pursue passions, take care of loved ones, and enjoy the freedom that comes with being fiscally secure.

Whether you're looking to add extra cushion to your current savings, plan for an early retirement, or simply understand how to make your money work harder for you, this book is designed to be your comprehensive guide. It's packed with actionable insights, motivational advice, and time-tested strategies to help you navigate the sometimes complex world of personal finance.

Throughout the chapters, we'll dive into various aspects of financial well-being—from understanding what financial independence truly means, to setting achievable financial goals, and mastering the art of budgeting and saving. We'll explore multiple income streams, delve into intelligent investing, and harness the power of compound interest to grow your wealth exponentially.

You'll also find invaluable information about retirement accounts, real estate investments, and tax strategies that can significantly enhance your financial position. We'll tackle insurance needs to protect what you've worked so hard to build and walk you through creating a tailor-made financial independence plan that's flexible yet robust enough to withstand life's uncertainties.

This book is thoughtfully crafted for those ready to take control of their financial futures. It's aimed at individuals between the ages of 30 and 67, who understand that now is the time to act. It doesn't matter if you're just starting out or looking to refine your existing strategies—this guide is inclusive and designed to meet you where you are.

As you read through each chapter, remember that financial independence isn't an unreachable dream; it's a tangible reality waiting for those who commit to the journey. Take the first step today, armed with knowledge, determination, and the readiness to transform your financial life forever.

Let's get started on this exciting path to financial freedom and wealth generation. Your future self will thank you.

Chapter 1: Understanding Financial Independence

Stepping into the world of financial independence is like embarking on a transformative journey. It's not just about accumulating wealth; it's about creating the freedom to live life on your own terms. At its core, financial independence means having sufficient income to cover your living expenses for the rest of your life without having to be employed or dependent on others.

Defining Financial Independence

So, what exactly does financial independence entail? In simple terms, it means having enough assets to generate income that exceeds your monthly expenses. This can come from various sources like investments, savings, or passive income streams. It's the moment when work becomes a choice rather than a necessity.

Imagine waking up each day knowing you have the freedom to pursue your passions, whether that's traveling the world, delving into hobbies, or spending quality time with loved ones. The essence of financial independence is about gaining control over your time and your life.

Benefits of Achieving Financial Independence

The advantages of reaching financial independence are numerous and profound. Here are some noteworthy benefits:

- **Stress Reduction:** Financial stress can affect every aspect of your life. Once you achieve financial independence, the anxiety about paying bills or losing a job diminishes significantly.
- **Increased Quality of Life:** With financial worries out of the way, you can focus on enhancing your overall quality of life. This could mean pursuing fulfilling activities, enjoying better health, and cultivating more meaningful relationships.
- **Empowerment and Freedom:** True financial independence provides a sense of empowerment. You have the liberty to make life choices without being constrained by financial limitations.
- **Early Retirement:** Many people aim for financial independence to retire early and enjoy their golden years without financial worries. This doesn't necessarily mean ceasing all productive activity but having the choice to slow down or change directions.

Achieving financial independence requires consistent planning, discipline, and sometimes sacrifices. Yet, the rewards make the journey worthwhile. Throughout this book, you'll find strategies, insights, and tools designed to help you reach this pivotal life goal.

Financial independence isn't just for a select few. Whether you're a young professional starting out, someone in the middle of your career, or nearing retirement, it's within your grasp. With focused effort and the right strategies, you too can unlock the door to financial independence and rewrite your financial future.

Ready to dive deeper? The next chapter will guide you through setting feasible financial goals, both short-term and long-term, to put you on the right path. Let's get started on this transformative journey together.

Defining Financial Independence

Financial independence is more than just a buzzword; it's a life-changing state that affords you the freedom to live on your own terms. At its core, financial independence means having sufficient personal wealth to live without needing to work actively for life's necessities. In other words, your assets generate enough income to cover your living expenses.

Let's break that down. Imagine waking up each day knowing that your bills are paid not because of the hours you clocked in at your job, but because the strategic financial choices you made are continuously working for you. Whether it's rental income from a property, dividends from stocks, or returns on other investments, the goal is to have income streams that don't require you to trade your time for money.

For many, financial independence means freedom from the anxiety of living paycheck to paycheck. It offers the luxury of choosing work that you're passionate about rather than work you have to do to meet ends. You're essentially buying back your time, affording you the opportunity to pursue dreams, hobbies, and experiences that enrich your life. Imagine the peace of mind and the sense of security that comes with knowing you're financially prepared for life's uncertainties.

However, achieving financial independence isn't about overnight success. It involves years of careful planning, disciplined saving, smart investing, and prudent spending. It demands understanding the intricate ways money can work for you, and then setting in motion strategies that align with your goals and risk tolerance.

We'll delve into the specifics of these strategies later, but right now, it's crucial to understand that financial independence is a scalable concept. What's important is determining what financial independence means for you personally. Your ideal lifestyle might differ from someone else's, and so will your financial needs. Whether it's the ability to travel the world or simply the comfort of a secure retirement, defining these goals is the first step towards achieving them.

So, as we move forward, think of financial independence as your personal journey. It's not just about having money; it's about life choices and the liberty to make them without undue financial constraints. In the following chapters, we'll explore how to set financial goals, create budgets, build diverse income streams, invest wisely, and protect your wealth—all aimed at guiding you toward your own path to financial independence.

Benefits of Achieving Financial Independence

Reaching financial independence isn't just about having a substantial amount of money in the bank; it's about transforming your entire lifestyle. When you achieve financial independence, you unlock a range of benefits that affect nearly every facet of your life, from stress levels to opportunities for personal growth.

First and foremost, financial independence reduces financial stress. Imagine not having to worry about paying your bills or dealing with unexpected expenses. Knowing that you have enough resources to cover your needs and wants brings an immense sense of relief and peace of mind. This reduction in financial anxiety can positively impact your mental and physical health, making it easier to enjoy life.

Another significant benefit is the freedom of choice. When you're financially independent, you gain the liberty to make decisions based on what you truly want, rather than what you can afford. This could mean pursuing a passion project, traveling, or spending more time with loved ones. It's about having the flexibility to design your life according to your values and interests.

Financial independence also opens doors to better opportunities. With a stable financial foundation, you can take calculated risks, such as starting a new business or investing in profitable ventures. Knowing that you have a safety net allows you to seize opportunities that others might shy away from due to financial constraints.

Additionally, achieving financial independence enables you to focus on personal development. When you're not constantly worrying about money, you can invest time and resources into learning new skills, pursuing hobbies, or even furthering your education. This continuous self-improvement can lead to a more fulfilling and enriched life.

Furthermore, financial independence provides the ability to give back. Whether it's supporting your family, donating to causes you care about, or volunteering your time, having the financial means allows you to make a more significant impact. You can contribute to the well-being of others, which can bring a deep sense of satisfaction and purpose.

Lastly, financial independence sets a powerful example for future generations. By demonstrating how to manage finances wisely and achieve stability, you can inspire and educate your children or younger relatives, helping them to avoid common financial pitfalls and encouraging them to strive for their own financial independence.

In summary, the benefits of achieving financial independence are wide-ranging and transformative. From reducing stress and gaining freedom of choice, to opening doors to new opportunities and enabling personal growth, financial independence is a goal worth striving for. Remember, it's about creating a life that aligns with your deepest values and desires, free from financial worry.

Chapter 2: Setting Financial Goals

Before diving into the depths of budgeting, investing, and income generation, it's crucial to have a clear idea of what you're working towards. Financial goals act as the beacon that guides you through your financial journey, ensuring that your efforts are aligned and purposeful. Setting these goals effectively is a foundational step in achieving financial independence.

Short-Term Goals

Short-term financial goals are the milestones you'll achieve within the next year. These goals can range from paying off a small debt to saving for a vacation or building an emergency fund. They are smaller, more immediate objectives that lay the groundwork for your long-term aspirations.

Start by identifying what you need to achieve within the next 12 months. Perhaps it's setting aside $500 for an emergency fund or paying off a credit card. Make sure these goals are specific and measurable. For example, "Save $2,000 for an emergency fund" is more actionable than a vague "Save money."

Once you've pinpointed your short-term objectives, break them down into manageable steps. If your goal is to save $2,000 in a year, aim to save around $167 each month. Adjust your spending habits and allocate portions of your income towards these goals. Document your progress regularly to stay motivated and on track.

Long-Term Goals

Long-term financial goals are usually set for periods extending beyond five years. These goals often revolve around significant life events such as buying a home, funding your children's education, or preparing for retirement. These objectives require more extensive planning and a deeper commitment.

First, define what you want to achieve in the long run. This could be something like "Accumulate $500,000 for retirement by age 65" or "Save $50,000 for a down payment on a home in five years." Your long-term goals should be ambitious yet realistic, inspiring you to stay diligent and disciplined.

Long-term goals necessitate strategic planning. You might need to delve into more sophisticated saving and investment strategies. Regularly contribute to retirement accounts such as 401(k)s or IRAs, invest in a diversified portfolio, and consider real estate as part of your long-term wealth generation plan. Regularly review and adjust your strategies based on changes in your life circumstances and financial markets.

To ensure these goals remain in focus, revisit them periodically. Life is unpredictable, and your objectives might need readjusting as you encounter new opportunities and challenges.

The Importance of Milestones

Setting financial milestones within your short-term and long-term goals can significantly enhance your progress. These milestones act as checkpoints, allowing you to evaluate how far you've come and what still needs attention. For instance, within a five-year savings plan for a home, set annual savings targets and celebrate each year's achievement. This not only motivates you but also gives you a clearer sense of your progress.

Balancing Short-Term and Long-Term Goals

One common mistake in setting financial goals is focusing too much on either the short-term or the long-term. It's vital to strike a balance. Allocate your resources in a way that allows immediate needs and future aspirations to be met concurrently. This balanced approach ensures steady progress and guards against the frustration of having to choose one over the other.

Remember, the path to financial independence is a continual journey. Setting clear, achievable goals equips you with the roadmap needed to traverse this journey successfully. Your financial goals should be a living document, evolving as you progress in your financial journey, encounter new experiences, and recalibrate your aspirations.

With your financial goals set, you're now prepared to delve into the nitty-gritty of budgeting and saving, the practical steps that transform your goals from mere aspirations to well-deserved realities.

Short-Term Goals

Setting short-term financial goals is a crucial step on your journey towards financial independence. Think of these as the building blocks that pave the way to achieving long-term wealth. Short-term goals typically span a timeframe of less than a year and are achievable without long-term commitment. They help build momentum and provide you with a roadmap to guide your longer-term financial strategy.

One of the first steps in setting short-term financial goals is identifying what you want to achieve imminently. These could range from establishing an emergency fund, paying off high-interest debt, saving for a family vacation, or even starting a side hustle to boost your income. The key is to be specific. Rather than saying "I want to save money," aim for something tangible like "I want to save $1,000 in the next six months."

Once you've identified these goals, it's time to break them down into actionable steps. This involves allocating resources, creating a detailed plan, and setting deadlines. For example, if your goal is to save $1,000 in six months, calculate how much you need to save each week or month to reach that target. This makes the goal less daunting and more manageable.

An essential part of this process is tracking your progress. Regularly review your financial goals to see how you're doing. Are you on track? Do you need to make adjustments? This is where budgeting tools and apps can come in handy, giving you a clear picture of your financial health and helping you stay accountable.

Being willing to course-correct is another important aspect of accomplishing short-term goals. Financial landscapes can change, unexpected expenses can arise, and personal circumstances can shift. If you find you're falling behind, evaluate why and adjust your approach. This flexibility ensures that setbacks don't derail your overall progress.

Lastly, it's important to celebrate your achievements. When you hit a short-term goal, take a moment to recognize your accomplishment. This not only provides motivation but reinforces positive financial habits. Small wins accumulate and build a foundation of confidence that you'll need as you move towards more ambitious, long-term financial goals.

Short-term financial goals might seem modest, but their impact can be profound. They ground your financial strategy in reality and give you the momentum to tackle more challenging financial milestones. By setting clear, achievable objectives and consistently working toward them, you're laying the groundwork for a future of financial stability and independence.

Long-Term Goals
When it comes to setting financial goals, thinking long term is crucial for true wealth generation and financial independence. While short-term goals might give you quick wins and boost your morale, it's the long-term ones that lay down the foundation for a financially secure future. Long-term financial goals typically include milestones such as buying a home, planning for retirement, or setting up a college fund for your children.

To begin with, clarity is key. Identify what you want to achieve in the long run and be specific about it. Rather than vaguely saying, "I want to retire comfortably," try to pinpoint the exact lifestyle you envision for yourself during retirement. Do you see yourself traveling the world, starting a small business, or perhaps moving to a tranquil countryside? The more precise you are, the better you can plan and execute your strategies.

Next, break down your long-term goals into manageable chunks. This approach helps transform seemingly insurmountable objectives into achievable targets. For example, if your goal is to amass $1 million by the time you're 65, you can work backward to determine how much you need to save and invest annually. This step-by-step plan gives you a clear roadmap and minimizes the feeling of being overwhelmed.

Consistency is another critical factor. Long-term financial goals often span decades, and achieving them requires steady commitment. Regularly contributing to your investment accounts or savings plans can be immensely powerful, especially when combined with the magic of compound interest. This leads us back to the idea of not just saving money but making your money work for you over time.

While on this journey, it's equally important to remain adaptable. Life is unpredictable, and your long-term goals might need recalibrating as circumstances change. Major life events such as marriage, the birth of a child, or career changes can all impact your financial objectives. Periodic reviews of your financial plan allow you to make necessary adjustments and stay on course.

Lastly, seek professional advice when needed. Financial advisers can provide invaluable insights and help tailor your investment strategies to meet your specific long-term goals. They bring a wealth of knowledge and experience that can guide you through complex financial landscapes, ensuring you make informed decisions.

Setting long-term financial goals might seem daunting, but with clear vision, consistent efforts, and the willingness to adapt, you can build a future rich in opportunities and financial security. Remember, the road to financial independence is a journey, and every step you take brings you closer to the life you've envisioned.

Chapter 3: Budgeting and Saving

When it comes to building wealth and achieving financial independence, budgeting and saving are fundamental elements that can't be overlooked. This chapter delves into practical techniques to manage your finances effectively and strategies to help you save more money over time. These principles will provide the foundation for all your other financial endeavors.

Effective Budgeting Techniques

Creating a budget might sound tedious, but it's an essential step toward financial freedom. A well-thought-out budget enables you to track your income and expenses, making it easier to identify areas where you can cut back and save. Here's how you can get started:

Effective Budgeting Techniques

When it comes to embarking on the journey towards financial independence, effective budgeting is one of the most powerful tools at your disposal. Mastering the art of budgeting not only helps you manage your current finances but also sets the stage for future wealth generation. Let's dive into some practical and proven techniques.

1. Track Every Dollar
The first step in effective budgeting is knowing exactly where your money goes. Keep tabs on every expense, no matter how small. This awareness is foundational; you can't manage what you don't measure. Tools like budgeting apps or simple spreadsheets can help you categorize and track expenses effortlessly.

2. Create a Spending Plan, Not a Budget
Think of your budget as a spending plan, guiding you on how to allocate your resources rather than limiting your choices. By framing it positively, you're more likely to stick to it. Prioritize essential expenses and allocate funds towards savings and investments before accounting for discretionary spending.

3. Use the 50/30/20 Rule
The 50/30/20 rule is a straightforward formula to manage your income: 50% goes to necessities like housing and food, 30% for discretionary expenses, and 20% towards savings and debt repayment. This balanced approach ensures you're covering your bases while also progressing towards your financial goals.

4. Automate Savings
Make saving effortless by automating transfers to your savings account or investment vehicles. Set up automatic deductions from your paycheck or bank account, ensuring you "pay yourself first" without the temptation to spend that money. This habit builds your nest egg steadily over time.

5. Review and Adjust Regularly
Your budget isn't set in stone. Life changes, and so should your budget. Regularly review your financial situation to adjust for any shifts in income, expenses, or financial goals. Monthly or quarterly check-ins can help you stay on track and make necessary changes promptly.

6. Cut Unnecessary Expenses
Identify and eliminate or reduce non-essential expenses. This can be anything from subscription services you rarely use to cutting down on dining out. Small savings in multiple areas can add up to significant amounts over time.

7. Use Cash for Discretionary Spending
Consider using cash for discretionary spending areas like entertainment or dining out. When you use cash, you're more likely to think twice before making a purchase. It gives you a tangible sense of how much you're spending, which credit cards often obscure.

8. Build an Emergency Fund
An emergency fund is your financial safety net, designed to cover unexpected expenses like medical bills or car repairs. Aim to save at least three to six months' worth of living expenses. This fund will prevent you from dipping into your savings or going into debt when the unexpected happens.

9. Prioritize Debt Repayment

High-interest debt can be a significant obstacle to financial independence. Focus on paying down debts as quickly as possible, starting with those that have the highest interest rates. This strategy minimizes the amount you pay in interest and frees up resources for savings and investments.

10. Celebrate Milestones

Recognize and celebrate when you hit financial milestones, whether it's paying off a credit card, building your emergency fund, or sticking to your spending plan for a designated period. These celebrations keep you motivated and committed to your financial journey.

By implementing these effective budgeting techniques, you'll lay a robust foundation for achieving financial independence and wealth generation. Remember, successful money management is about making conscious decisions and being consistent with your practices. Each step you take brings you closer to financial freedom.

Strategies for Saving Money

Saving money often feels like an uphill battle, but with the right strategies, it can become a seamless part of your financial routine. In this section, we'll delve into practical methods that you can implement today to enhance your savings. Remember, every small step you take moves you closer to achieving financial independence.

First and foremost, let's talk about automating your savings. Set up automatic transfers from your checking account to a dedicated savings or investment account. By doing this, you essentially "pay yourself first." It's an effortless way to save regularly without having to think about it each month. Many banks and financial apps provide easy ways to automate these transfers, so take advantage of them.

Next, consider implementing the 50/30/20 rule. This budgeting rule suggests that you allocate 50% of your income to needs, 30% to wants, and 20% to savings and debt repayment. It's a straightforward guideline that can help you prioritize your spending and maximize your savings rate. Tailor the percentages as needed to fit your specific financial situation.

Take time to audit your subscriptions and memberships. Often, we sign up for services and forget about them, even if we're no longer using them. Review your bank statements at least once a quarter and cancel any subscriptions or memberships that no longer serve you. This can free up a surprising amount of money over time.

Another effective strategy is to embrace the concept of delayed gratification. When you're tempted to make an impulse purchase, give yourself a cooling-off period. Wait 24 hours or even a week before deciding whether to buy the item. More often than not, you'll find that the impulse subsides, and you can save that money instead.

Cutting down on non-essential expenses can also significantly boost your savings. Simple changes like cooking at home instead of dining out, or cutting back on premium cable packages, can add up. Look for areas in your monthly expenses where you can make small adjustments, and funnel those savings into your investment or savings accounts.

Don't forget to take advantage of deals and discounts. Use cashback apps, coupon codes, and loyalty programs. When shopping for necessities, these tools can help you save a considerable amount over time. Just ensure that you're not buying things you don't need simply because there's a discount.

Lastly, build an emergency fund that can cover three to six months of living expenses. This will give you peace of mind and prevent you from dipping into your long-term savings or going into debt in case of unexpected expenses. It's a safety net that everyone should have.

By incorporating these strategies into your daily life, you're not just saving money—you're setting the stage for financial freedom. These are practical, actionable steps you can take starting today. Understand that saving money isn't about depriving yourself; it's about making conscious choices that align with your larger financial goals. Every penny saved is a step closer to wealth generation and financial security.

Chapter 4: Income Streams

As you navigate the path to financial independence, understanding and cultivating multiple income streams is essential. While traditional employment income forms the bedrock for many, diversifying beyond a single source can significantly enhance your financial stability and growth. This chapter delves into various income avenues, explaining how to harness each to bolster your wealth generation strategy.

Traditional Employment Income

For most people, their primary source of income comes from traditional employment. This includes salaries, wages, and bonuses from your employer. The predictability and steadiness of a paycheck provide a sense of security. However, relying solely on this can be risky, given economic fluctuations and job market unpredictability.

Your first step should be maximizing your earnings in your current career. Seek opportunities for advancement, negotiate raises, or even consider additional training or education to boost your qualifications. Higher earnings in your primary job can provide seed money for other income-generating ventures.

Passive Income Sources

Passive income is the Holy Grail for many aspiring to financial freedom. It's money you earn with minimal ongoing effort. Think of it as your finances working for you. Below, we explore some potent passive income sources.

Real Estate Investments

Real estate has long been a preferred method for generating passive income. Whether you're renting out residential properties or investing in commercial real estate, the income potential is substantial. Rental properties can provide consistent monthly income, and over time, the property value can appreciate, offering long-term wealth growth.

To get started, consider the location and type of property. Look for areas with steady demand, good infrastructure, and potential for appreciation. You might also explore real estate investment trusts (REITs) if direct property management isn't appealing to you.

Dividend Stocks

Investing in dividend-paying stocks is another effective way to cultivate passive income. Dividend stocks provide regular payouts based on the company's profits. These payments can be a reliable income source, especially when you diversify across various companies and sectors.

To begin, research and select companies with a history of consistent dividend payouts. Consider using dividend reinvestment plans (DRIPs) to compound your returns by automatically purchasing additional shares with your dividends.

Online Businesses

The digital age has opened up myriad opportunities for generating passive income through online businesses. These can range from e-commerce stores and affiliate marketing to online courses and content creation. The initial effort in setting up these ventures can pay off significantly over time.

Identify a niche you're passionate about or have expertise in. Develop quality content, products, or services that address a gap or need in that niche. With consistent effort and strategic marketing, online businesses can develop into lucrative passive income sources.

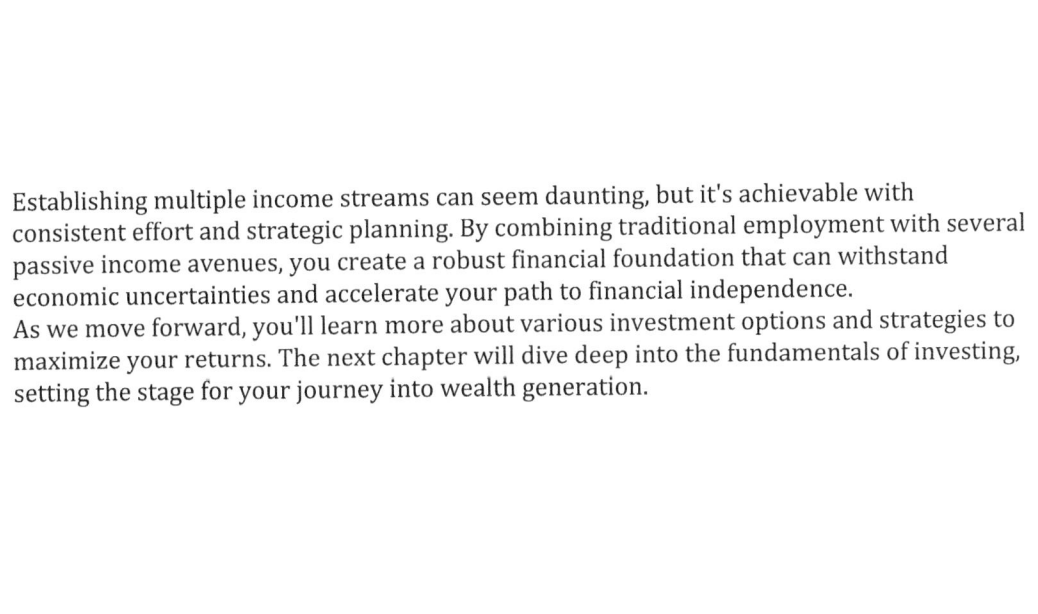

Establishing multiple income streams can seem daunting, but it's achievable with consistent effort and strategic planning. By combining traditional employment with several passive income avenues, you create a robust financial foundation that can withstand economic uncertainties and accelerate your path to financial independence.

As we move forward, you'll learn more about various investment options and strategies to maximize your returns. The next chapter will dive deep into the fundamentals of investing, setting the stage for your journey into wealth generation.

Traditional Employment Income

Traditional employment income is probably the most familiar source of earnings for many people. This type of income stems from working a job where you trade your time and skills for a salary or hourly wage. Whether you're an employee of a company, a government worker, or working in the not-for-profit sector, this is the kind of income that offers a regular paycheck, usually accompanied by benefits such as health insurance, retirement plans, and paid time off.

The advantage of traditional employment income lies in its stability and predictability. Knowing that a certain amount of money will hit your bank account every two weeks or at the end of the month can provide a sense of security and make budgeting easier. Additionally, traditional employment often provides opportunities for professional growth, skill development, and career advancement. Climbing the corporate ladder or transitioning into higher-paying roles within your field can significantly increase your earning potential.

Nevertheless, relying solely on traditional employment income has its downsides. For one, you're limited by the number of hours you can work each week, capping your potential income. Also, this income is generally subject to federal, state, and possibly local taxes, which can take a substantial bite out of your earnings. Furthermore, job security can be tenuous; layoffs, downsizing, or company closures can disrupt your income stream unexpectedly.

It's essential to maximize the benefits of traditional employment income while acknowledging its limitations. Negotiating your salary and benefits package is crucial. Don't hesitate to ask for what you're worth during hiring or performance reviews. Additionally, focusing on skill enhancement and professional development can lead to promotions and increased wages. Pursuing certifications, attending workshops, or even going back to school part-time are all strategies to boost your employability and earning power.

Understanding the role traditional employment income plays in your financial portfolio is the first step. While it's a cornerstone for many, it shouldn't be the only source of income you rely on if your goal is financial independence. Diversifying your income streams, which we'll discuss in the following sections, can provide greater financial security and help you achieve your wealth generation goals.

Passive Income Sources

When it comes to generating wealth and achieving financial independence, passive income can play a pivotal role. Unlike traditional employment income, which requires trading your time for money, passive income streams offer the promise of earning money with minimal ongoing effort. This section will explore various sources of passive income, helping you to create a diversified and resilient financial foundation.

Passive income is not about getting rich quick; it's about building a portfolio of income streams that grow and generate cash flow over time. This gradual wealth-building process requires strategic planning, initial effort, and sometimes a bit of capital. The key is to find opportunities that align with your financial goals and risk tolerance.

First, consider **real estate investments**. Owning rental property can be one of the most reliable ways to generate passive income. The idea is simple: you purchase a property, rent it out to tenants, and collect monthly rent checks. It's a tried and true method, but does require initial capital, ongoing maintenance, and property management. The beauty of real estate investments is their potential for appreciation, tax benefits, and consistent rental income. We'll delve deeper into this in Chapter 9, but for now, keep in mind that real estate can be a cornerstone of your passive income strategy.

Next, think about **dividend stocks**. When you invest in dividend-paying companies, you earn a portion of the company's profits on a regular basis, typically quarterly. This can become a significant income stream, especially as you invest more and the dividends compound over time. The stock market does fluctuate, so it's important to choose well-established, financially sound companies. Chapter 5 will address the intricacies of investing in stocks, but the foundation is knowing that dividends can provide a steady cash flow.

Another avenue to explore is **online businesses**. The internet offers numerous opportunities to create passive income. Think about e-commerce stores, digital products, and affiliate marketing. These ventures may require upfront work to set up, but once operational, they can generate income with minimal ongoing effort. For instance, creating an online course or writing an eBook allows you to earn money long after the initial upload. While the effort to create meaningful content can be substantial at the onset, the potential for ongoing revenue is significant. We'll go into more detail on this topic in Chapter 4.

Diversifying your income streams is crucial. Relying on one source of income can be risky, so spreading your investments across different types of passive income can provide more stability and security. As you build these various streams, they work together to enhance your financial independence and wealth-building efforts.

Remember, passive income doesn't mean 'no work'. Initially, you'll need to invest time, effort, and sometimes money to set up these income sources. However, the goal is that over time, the income generated requires less and less active involvement from you. By incorporating passive income into your overall financial strategy, you'll be setting yourself up to achieve greater financial freedom and security.

As we proceed in this book, you'll learn about specific strategies and tools to optimize these passive income sources. Take the time to explore these options, consider which align best with your goals, and make a plan to integrate them into your financial journey. Passive income can be a powerful step toward securing your financial future.

Real Estate Investments are a cornerstone for many when it comes to wealth generation and financial independence. Real estate offers not only the potential for substantial returns but also the tangibility and security many investors find appealing. Let's dive into why this asset class can be a game-changer for your financial journey.

Investing in real estate goes beyond just purchasing a home to live in. While homeownership can be a stable foundation, it's the additional investment properties that can truly accelerate your wealth. One key benefit is the potential for passive income through rental properties. Imagine earning a steady income every month, even while you sleep. Leveraging rental income can make a tremendous impact on achieving financial independence sooner rather than later.

Another compelling reason for investing in real estate is appreciation. Historically, real estate values tend to increase over time. This means that the property you buy today could be worth significantly more a few years down the line. The dual advantage of rental income and property appreciation makes real estate an attractive investment.

Let's not overlook the tax benefits associated with real estate investments. As a property owner, you can write off various expenses against your income, such as mortgage interest, property taxes, repairs, and maintenance. These deductions can significantly reduce your taxable income, resulting in more money in your pocket.

Real estate also offers a unique advantage through leverage. By using borrowed capital (like a mortgage) to finance the investment, you can earn a return on a much larger asset base than if you were using just your own money. This strategy can magnify your returns, albeit with some added risk, which needs to be managed carefully.

In addition to residential real estate, commercial real estate can be an equally lucrative avenue. This includes office buildings, retail spaces, and industrial properties. These investments generally come with longer lease terms and higher rental yields, although they might require a more significant initial outlay and a deeper understanding of the market.

It's important to note that while real estate has many upsides, it isn't without its challenges. Market fluctuations, property management headaches, and unexpected expenses can all impact your returns. However, with careful planning and due diligence, the benefits can far outweigh the downsides.

In conclusion, real estate investments can play a crucial role in your financial independence plan. Whether it's generating passive income, enjoying tax benefits, or leveraging property appreciation, real estate provides a flexible and potentially profitable pathway to building lasting wealth. Take the first step by educating yourself, analyzing the market, and making informed decisions. The journey to financial independence is paved with smart investments, and real estate can be one of the most powerful tools in your arsenal.

Dividend Stocks are like the unsung heroes of wealth generation, especially when you're looking to create a steady stream of passive income. Imagine owning shares in a company and getting paid just for holding on to them. That's essentially what dividend stocks offer— a portion of the company's earnings distributed to shareholders at regular intervals. It's a concept as old as investing itself, but its power is often underestimated.

What makes dividend stocks particularly appealing to our age group is their dual capability to provide immediate income and potential for long-term growth. While the stock price may fluctuate over time, those dividend payments can be a reliable source of cash flow to supplement your primary income or fund your retirement. The beauty of this is that you're essentially getting paid to wait.

In terms of selecting the right dividend stocks, it's crucial to focus on companies with a history of consistent and increasing payments. These companies are often well-established and financially stable, making them less risky than growth stocks. You're not looking for the next big tech startup here; you're seeking enterprises with a proven track record.

Balancing your portfolio with a mix of dividend-paying stocks from different sectors can also help mitigate risk. Diversification ensures that even if one industry faces a downturn, the others can keep your income stream stable. Think of it as not putting all your eggs in one basket.

Compounding is another key element to consider. Reinvesting your dividends into more shares of the same stock can exponentially grow your investment over time. This strategy can significantly increase your wealth, especially when combined with the power of compound interest discussed in earlier chapters.

To illustrate, let's say you own 100 shares of a company that pays an annual dividend of $2 per share. That's $200 a year. If you reinvest those dividends to buy more shares, next year's dividend will apply to the increased number of shares, creating a snowball effect. Over several years, this can lead to a substantial increase in both the number of shares you own and the dividends you receive.

Avoiding high-yield traps is equally important. A high dividend yield might seem attractive at first glance, but it can also be a red flag indicating that the company is in trouble. Always research the company's financial health, payout ratios, and market position. Look for sustainability rather than just high yields.

So, what's the takeaway here? Dividend stocks can be a game-changer in your journey to financial independence. They offer a potent mix of income and growth potential, backed by the stability of established companies. Whether you're just starting out or looking to diversify your portfolio, dividend stocks can provide a reliable foundation to build upon. Take the time to choose wisely, reinvest strategically, and watch how this seemingly simple investment can contribute to your wealth-building efforts.

Online Businesses have exploded in popularity, offering unprecedented opportunities for wealth generation. Whether you're looking to supplement your income or completely replace your traditional employment, an online business can be a viable pathway to financial independence.

The beauty of *online businesses* lies in their flexibility. You can start a side hustle while maintaining your day job, and potentially scale it into a full-time venture. From ecommerce and digital products to service-based businesses and affiliate marketing, there are a myriad of options to suit your skills and interests.

Let's consider ecommerce. Selling products online through platforms like Amazon or your own website can generate substantial income. With the rise of dropshipping, you don't even need to worry about inventory or shipping. Instead, you focus on marketing and managing your online store.

For those with expertise in a specific field, offering **digital services** can be highly lucrative. Whether it's consulting, coaching, or freelancing, the internet makes it easier than ever to reach a global audience. Websites like Upwork and Fiverr can connect you with clients looking for your skills.

Affiliate marketing is another excellent avenue. By promoting other people's products and earning a commission for every sale made through your referral, you're effectively getting paid to share recommendations. This can be done through blogs, social media, or YouTube channels.

If you have a knack for creating digital products, consider developing ebooks, online courses, or software. These products can generate passive income long after they've been launched. Once created, they can be sold repeatedly without the need for ongoing production costs.

Diversification is key. Don't rely on a single source of income. Explore different *online business models* and identify which ones resonate with you and your audience. The initial investment in time and effort can pay off massively in the long run.

The freedom and potential that online businesses offer are unparalleled. They allow you to work from anywhere, set your own schedule, and, most importantly, build a scalable source of income. Embrace the digital era and take the first step towards financial independence by exploring the world of online businesses.

Chapter 5: Investments

So, you've honed in on your financial goals, mastered budgeting, and explored various income streams. Now, it's time to discuss investments—a cornerstone of any robust wealth-building strategy. This chapter unpacks the fundamentals of investing and highlights the types of investments that can accelerate your journey toward financial independence.

Basics of Investing

Investing is the act of allocating money into assets or ventures with the expectation of generating income or profit. Simply put, it's about making your money work for you. Understanding the basics involves grasping the key principles of risk and return. The higher the potential return, the higher the risk. However, balanced and informed decision-making can help mitigate these risks.

Compound interest is one of the most powerful tools in investing, and we'll dive deeper into this in the next chapter. For now, know this: the sooner you start investing, the more time your money has to grow exponentially. Think of investment as planting a tree—the best time to plant it was yesterday; the second-best time is today.

Types of Investments

Diversification is an essential principle in investment strategy. It's about spreading your investments across various asset classes to reduce risk. Some common types of investments include:

- **Stocks:** Buying shares in a company makes you a part-owner of that company. The value of your investment rises or falls with the company's success. Stocks can offer high returns but come with increased volatility.
- **Bonds:** Essentially loans you give to a corporation or government. They pay you back with interest over time. Bonds are typically less risky than stocks and provide steady income.
- **Mutual Funds:** A collective pool of money from many investors used to buy a diversified portfolio of stocks, bonds, or other securities. Managed by professionals, mutual funds offer diversification and professional oversight but come with management fees.
- **ETFs (Exchange-Traded Funds):** Similar to mutual funds but traded like a stock on an exchange. They often have lower fees and provide instant diversification.

Each of these investment types has unique characteristics, benefits, and drawbacks. The key is not to put all your eggs in one basket. Spread your investments across various assets to cushion potential losses and position yourself for long-term success.

Start with understanding your risk tolerance—how much risk you're willing to take on for the potential of higher returns. Next, consider your investment horizon—or the amount of time you have to invest before needing to access the money. These factors will guide you in choosing the right mix of investments.

Why Invest?

Why should you dive into the world of investments? Simply because savings alone won't cut it. Inflation decreases the purchasing power of your money over time. To outpace inflation and grow your wealth, you need investments that offer returns higher than the inflation rate.

Consider this an opportunity rather than a necessity. With the right approach, investing becomes a powerful venue for achieving financial freedom—be it through funding your retirement, providing for education, or simply creating more security for your future.

In the chapters ahead, we'll delve into the power of compound interest, retirement accounts, tax strategies, and more. We'll guide you step-by-step, ensuring you're well-equipped to make informed and confident investment decisions.

Remember, every journey starts with a single step. Don't wait—begin your investment journey today, and let your money start working for you.

Basics of Investing
Investing is a powerful tool in your journey toward financial independence and wealth creation. At its core, investing involves allocating money into various assets or ventures with the expectation of generating a return. While the concept itself is straightforward, mastering investing requires a solid understanding of some foundational principles. Let's break down the essentials.

Understand Your Financial Situation
Before diving into the intricacies of investing, it's crucial to have a clear picture of your current financial status. Assess your income, expenses, debts, and savings. This step is essential because it helps determine how much you can afford to invest without compromising your financial stability. A detailed budget can be an excellent tool for this purpose.

Set Clear Investment Goals
Every successful investment strategy begins with clearly defined goals. Ask yourself what you aim to achieve with your investments. Are you saving for retirement, building an emergency fund, or looking to purchase a home? Knowing your objectives will guide your investment choices and help you stay focused.

Understand Risk Tolerance
Investing inherently involves risk, and it's vital to understand your risk tolerance. This refers to your ability and willingness to endure market fluctuations. Generally, investments with higher potential returns come with higher risks. Evaluate your comfort level and financial capacity to handle potential losses. This self-awareness will help you choose suitable investment options.

Diversification
Diversification is an investing principle that mitigates risk by spreading your investments across various asset classes. Instead of putting all your eggs in one basket, you invest in a mix of stocks, bonds, mutual funds, and other assets. This strategy reduces the impact of a poor-performing investment on your overall portfolio.

Start Early and Be Consistent
The earlier you begin investing, the more time your money has to grow. The power of compound interest means that even small, regular contributions can accumulate significantly over time. Consistency is key. Make investing a habit, just like saving, and stick with it.

Educate Yourself
Knowledge is power in the world of investing. Take the time to educate yourself about different types of investments and market trends. Financial news, books, and seminars can be excellent resources. The more informed you are, the better decisions you'll make.

Stay Patient and Avoid Emotional Decisions
Investing is a long-term endeavor, and it's essential to stay patient. Market fluctuations are normal, and knee-jerk reactions can be detrimental. Avoid making impulsive decisions based on short-term market movements. Remember, investing is about the long game.

Review and Adjust Your Portfolio

Your financial goals and situation may change over time, so it's important to review your investment portfolio regularly. Assess its performance and make adjustments as needed. This proactive approach ensures that your investments remain aligned with your goals. By grasping these fundamentals, you'll be well on your way to becoming a savvy investor. Whether you're just starting or looking to refine your strategy, mastering the basics can significantly enhance your financial future.

Types of Investments

Venturing into the world of investments can be both exciting and daunting, especially if you haven't done it before. The types of investments you choose can significantly influence your journey towards financial independence. Understanding these helps make informed decisions and minimize risks. Let's dive into the four main types of investments that we'll explore in this book: stocks, bonds, mutual funds, and ETFs.

Stocks: Stocks represent ownership in a company. When you buy a stock, you're buying a piece of that company. As a shareholder, you might benefit from dividends and potential appreciation in the stock's price. Stocks are known for their high potential returns, but they also come with a higher level of risk. Market fluctuations can be volatile, which means you could see significant gains but also substantial losses.

Bonds: Bonds are essentially loans you give to corporations or governments. In return, the issuer agrees to pay back the principal amount on a set date and makes periodic interest payments. They're considered safer than stocks because they offer more predictable returns. However, they generally provide lower returns compared to stocks. Bond investments can be a great way to add stability to your portfolio.

Mutual Funds: Mutual funds pool money from multiple investors to buy a diversified portfolio of stocks, bonds, or other securities. This allows you to invest in a broader range of assets without having to manage each investment individually. Mutual funds are managed by professional fund managers, making them a good option for those looking for expert guidance. They can offer stability through diversification, although they might come with management fees that can eat into your returns.

ETFs (Exchange-Traded Funds): ETFs operate somewhat like mutual funds but are traded on stock exchanges. They combine the diversification benefits of mutual funds with the trading flexibility of stocks. This means you can buy and sell ETF shares throughout the trading day at market price, which can be advantageous in a rapidly changing market. ETFs often have lower fees than mutual funds and can be a cost-effective way to build a diverse investment portfolio.

Each type of investment has its own set of characteristics, benefits, and drawbacks. The right mix for you depends on your financial goals, risk tolerance, and investment horizon. In the following sections, we'll dive deeper into these investment types to help you make the best choices on your path to financial independence.

Stocks are often regarded as the cornerstone of any robust investment portfolio. When you're looking to achieve financial independence or generate wealth, it's essential to understand what stocks are, how they work, and why they can be a powerful tool for your financial journey.

At their core, stocks represent ownership in a company. When you buy a stock, you are essentially purchasing a tiny piece of that company. The value of your stock is tied to the company's performance and market perception. If the company does well, your stock's value can increase, potentially providing substantial returns.

The beauty of investing in stocks lies in their versatility. From blue-chip companies that offer stability to growth stocks with the potential for enormous gains, you have a wide array of options. Remember, diversification is crucial. By investing in a variety of stocks, you can mitigate risk and create a balanced portfolio. This way, the poor performance of one stock won't heavily impact your overall investments.

For those new to stock investing, it's vital to start with a sound strategy. Begin by researching and understanding the market, then consider investing in companies with strong fundamentals and a proven track record. Common strategies include value investing, where you look for undervalued stocks, and growth investing, where you focus on companies with significant potential for expansion.

One of the significant advantages of stocks is the potential for both capital appreciation and dividend income. Dividends are regular payouts companies offer to shareholders, often providing a steady income stream. By reinvesting these dividends, you can harness the power of compound interest, amplifying your returns over time.

However, investing in stocks is not without its risks. Market volatility can cause stock prices to fluctuate, sometimes dramatically. It's crucial to stay informed, be patient, and keep a long-term perspective. Emotional decisions driven by market highs and lows can often lead to poor investment choices.

A practical approach to managing your stock investments includes setting clear financial goals, continually educating yourself, and regularly reviewing your portfolio. Don't hesitate to seek advice from financial advisors who can offer personalized insights based on your unique financial situation.

The world of stocks is vast and ever-evolving, providing numerous opportunities to grow your wealth. With careful planning, informed choices, and a bit of patience, stocks can play a pivotal role in your path to financial independence.

Bonds offer a fascinating blend of stability and income, making them a crucial component of a well-diversified investment portfolio. Unlike stocks, which represent ownership in a company, bonds are essentially loans you make to corporations or governments. When you purchase a bond, you are lending money to the issuer in exchange for periodic interest payments and the return of the bond's face value when it matures.

Think of bonds as the "bread and butter" of a balanced investment strategy. While they might not provide the adrenaline rush of high-flying stocks, they serve a vital role in mitigating risk and providing steady, predictable returns. Especially for those approaching retirement, bonds can offer a reliable income stream, preserving capital while still contributing to overall growth.

The beauty of bonds lies in their flexibility and variety. There are government bonds, known for their low risk and stable returns. Corporate bonds, on the other hand, offer higher yields but come with increased risk. Municipal bonds offer tax benefits, making them an attractive option for high-net-worth individuals looking to maximize tax efficiency.

A key feature of bonds is their interest payments, known as coupon payments. These are typically paid semi-annually and provide a steady income stream. The frequency and reliability of these payments can be particularly appealing if you're seeking stability in your investment portfolio. Regular income can make bonds an excellent tool for meeting financial goals, especially those related to retirement planning and wealth preservation.

It's also essential to understand the relationship between bond prices and interest rates. When interest rates rise, bond prices generally fall, and vice versa. This inverse relationship can impact the value of your bond holdings, but it also creates opportunities. For example, in a rising interest rate environment, newly issued bonds will offer higher yields, making them an attractive investment.

Diversification within bonds is equally important. Holding a mix of government, corporate, and municipal bonds, as well as bonds with varying maturities, can further reduce risk and enhance returns. By spreading your investments across different types of bonds, you can better withstand market fluctuations and economic uncertainties.

Incorporating bonds into your investment strategy is not just about stability; it's also about strategic growth. They act as a financial anchor, providing resilience against market downturns. Their relatively low volatility makes them a prudent choice, particularly for investors with a lower risk tolerance.

Ultimately, bonds are about balance. They allow you to ride the wave of market volatility while still enjoying a steady, dependable income. This balance is particularly crucial during times of economic uncertainty, where the safety and reliability of bonds become ever more apparent. As you move forward in your financial journey, remember that bonds can be the cornerstone that supports your wealth-building efforts, providing both security and growth.

Mutual Funds offer a fantastic opportunity for individuals looking to invest without needing to become experts in selecting individual stocks or bonds. If you've ever found yourself overwhelmed by the sheer volume of investment choices or the complexities involved in managing your portfolio, mutual funds might just be the solution you're looking for.

So, what exactly are mutual funds? At their core, mutual funds pool money from various investors to purchase a diversified portfolio of stocks, bonds, or other securities. This diversification lowers the risk, as your investment isn't tied to the performance of a single asset. It's a bit like a financial safety net, spreading the risk across a wider array of investments while simplifying the management process.

Now, let's talk about the advantages of investing in mutual funds. First and foremost, they provide instant diversification. Imagine having a piece of several companies across different sectors rather than putting all your eggs in one basket. This diversification can significantly reduce the volatility of your investment, making your financial journey a bit smoother.

Another compelling benefit is professional management. Mutual funds are overseen by experienced portfolio managers who make informed decisions about which assets to buy and sell. This hands-on management can be particularly beneficial for those who don't have the time or expertise to do the heavy lifting themselves. You're essentially leveraging the expertise of professionals whose full-time job is to navigate the investment landscape.

Furthermore, mutual funds come in a variety of types to suit different investment goals and risk tolerances. Whether you're looking for aggressive growth, steady income, or a balanced approach, there's likely a mutual fund designed to meet your needs. From equity funds focusing on stocks, to bond funds providing more stable returns, and even balanced funds that mix both, you have options to align with your financial objectives.

Mutual funds also offer ease of access and liquidity. Unlike some other investment vehicles that might lock up your money for extended periods, mutual funds typically allow you to buy or sell shares at the end of each trading day. This flexibility is particularly advantageous if you need access to your capital on relatively short notice.

However, it's not all sunshine and roses. There are some considerations to keep in mind. Management fees can eat into your returns, especially with actively managed funds. It's crucial to understand the fee structure before you commit. Additionally, not all mutual funds perform equally. Historical performance, the reputation of the management team, and the fund's expense ratio are factors you should evaluate.

Incorporating mutual funds into your investment strategy can play a pivotal role in achieving financial independence. By providing diversification, professional management, and adaptable investment options, mutual funds offer a pathway to growth while mitigating risk. It's about making your money work for you efficiently and effectively, setting the stage for achieving your financial dreams.

ETFs are an intriguing and versatile investment vehicle that deserves your attention as you embark on your journey to financial independence. You're probably familiar with stocks and mutual funds, but ETFs—or Exchange-Traded Funds—combine aspects of both, creating a unique investment option that's both accessible and potentially lucrative.

At their core, ETFs are essentially collections of various assets, such as stocks, bonds, or commodities, bundled together into a single fund. This collection offers diversification, reducing your risk because your investment is spread across multiple assets rather than being concentrated in one place. Imagine you're building a diversified portfolio but without the headache of buying individual stocks and bonds. ETFs do that heavy lifting for you.

One of the most appealing features of ETFs is their simplicity and ease of access. Unlike mutual funds, which are priced once a day, ETFs trade on stock exchanges, just like regular stocks. This means you can buy and sell ETFs throughout the trading day, giving you greater flexibility and control over your investments. Whether you're a novice investor or more experienced, the liquidity and transparency of ETFs make them a compelling choice.

Now, let's talk about costs. Many ETFs come with much lower expense ratios compared to mutual funds. These lower costs can significantly impact your returns over time, as fewer fees mean more of your money is working for you. Also, because ETFs aim to replicate the performance of a specific index rather than outperform it, they tend to engage in less frequent trading, which further diminishes cost through lower transaction fees.

ETFs also offer various investment strategies tailored to your unique financial goals. Interested in tech stocks? There's an ETF for that. Want exposure to international markets or emerging industries? ETFs have you covered. This flexibility allows you to tailor your portfolio to align with your risk tolerance, interests, and long-term objectives. As you delve deeper into financial independence, having a mix of ETFs can play a crucial role in your overall investment strategy.

Additionally, for those of you already working with retirement accounts like a 401k or an IRA, ETFs can often be included in these plans. This compatibility makes them an excellent option for diversifying your retirement portfolio, helping to ensure that you're not overly reliant on a single asset class as you work towards your golden years.

There's also an inherent motivational aspect to consider with ETFs. They simplify the investment process, allowing you to take more control over your financial future without needing extensive financial expertise. This ease of use can inspire greater confidence and encourage you to take the necessary steps toward reaching your financial goals.

ETFs, with their robust combination of diversification, low costs, flexibility, and accessibility, are a powerful tool in your investment arsenal. They're not only an efficient way to grow your wealth but also provide the added peace of mind that comes from knowing your investments are well-balanced and strategically diversified. As you progress on your path to financial independence, consider how ETFs can fit into and strengthen your overall investment strategy.

Chapter 6: The Power of Compound Interest

Welcome to Chapter 6, where we delve into one of the most fundamental yet incredibly powerful concepts in wealth generation: compound interest. You might have heard Albert Einstein's famous quote calling compound interest the "eighth wonder of the world." It's an idea so simple yet so profound that understanding it can change your financial future.

Understanding Compound Interest

Before diving into strategies to maximize compound interest, let's take a moment to grasp what it is. At its core, compound interest is the interest you earn on both your original investment and the interest that has been added to it over time. This "interest on interest" effect creates a snowball effect, where your wealth grows faster and faster as time goes on. Imagine you have $1,000 and it earns an annual interest rate of 5%. In the first year, you would make $50, bringing your total to $1,050. In the second year, you earn interest not just on the $1,000 but also on the $50 you earned last year. This means you'll earn $52.50, making your new total $1,102.50. Over time, this compounding effect can turn modest savings into substantial wealth.

Maximizing Compound Interest

Now that you understand the basics, let's explore how you can make compound interest work harder for you. Here are some strategies to consider:

- **Start Early:** The sooner you begin investing, the more time your money has to grow. Even small amounts invested early can lead to significant gains down the line. Consider this: investing $5,000 a year starting at age 25 versus starting at age 35 could mean a difference of hundreds of thousands of dollars by retirement.
- **Be Consistent:** Regular, consistent investments are key. Whether it's through automatic payroll deductions into a 401k or setting up an automatic transfer to a savings account, consistency helps maintain the compounding effect.
- **Reinvest Your Earnings:** Make sure that any dividends, interest, or earnings are reinvested rather than spent. Reinvestment fuels the compounding engine and accelerates your wealth growth.
- **Choose High-Interest Accounts:** While safer options like savings accounts and certificates of deposit (CDs) offer modest interest rates, exploring higher-yielding options like stocks, bonds, and mutual funds can substantially increase your returns over time.
- **Be Patient:** The real magic of compound interest is seen over the long term. While it's tempting to dip into your savings for immediate needs, patience is essential. The longer you let your investments compound, the greater your wealth will grow.

By implementing these strategies, you can harness the power of compound interest to build lasting wealth and work toward financial independence. Remember, time and consistency are your best allies in this journey. The beauty of compound interest lies in its

simplicity and effectiveness, making it an indispensable tool in your path to financial freedom.
So, as you take control of your financial future, keep the power of compound interest in mind. It's not just a financial principle; it's a key that can unlock the door to a more prosperous and secure life.

Understanding Compound Interest

If there's one concept in finance that truly holds the power to transform your wealth, it's compound interest. You might have heard it said: "Compound interest is the eighth wonder of the world." This isn't just a catchy phrase; the financial principles behind it have stood the test of time, allowing many to grow their fortunes steadily and reliably. Let's dive into what makes compound interest so powerful.

At its core, compound interest is the interest on a loan or deposit calculated based on both the initial principal and the accumulated interest from previous periods. In simpler terms, it's "interest on interest," and this leads to exponential growth over time. Unlike simple interest, which is only calculated on the principal amount, compound interest considers both your initial investment and the interest that accumulates on it.

To illustrate, imagine you invest $1,000 at an annual interest rate of 5%, compounded yearly. At the end of the first year, you'd earn $50 in interest, bringing your total to $1,050. In the second year, you don't just earn interest on your initial $1,000; you also earn interest on the $50 interest from the first year. This process repeats, causing your investment to grow faster each year.

Time is the key ingredient that magnifies the power of compound interest. The longer you let your money grow, the more impressive the results. This is why starting early is often emphasized in personal finance. Even small investments can grow substantially given enough time. Conversely, delaying investment can significantly reduce the potential returns, making it crucial to begin as soon as possible.

But compound interest isn't just about earning. It also applies to debts and can lead to financial pitfalls if not managed wisely. High-interest debts like credit card balances can compound against you, causing the amount owed to balloon over time. This is why it's essential to understand both sides of compound interest – how it can work for you and against you.

In summary, the magic of compound interest lies in its ability to accelerate your financial growth through the reinvestment of earnings. Whether you're looking to build a retirement nest egg or simply grow your savings, leveraging compound interest can help you achieve your financial goals more effectively. Stay tuned as we explore ways to maximize this powerful tool in the next section.

Maximizing Compound Interest

To truly harness the power of compound interest, it's crucial to understand not just how it works, but how you can strategically maximize its potential. Here are several actionable strategies that can help you make the most of compound interest, ultimately accelerating your journey to financial independence.

Start Early

Time is your greatest ally when it comes to maximizing compound interest. The earlier you start investing, the more time your money has to grow. Even modest contributions can grow significantly over decades. For instance, starting to invest in your 20s gives your investments a longer horizon to benefit from the magic of compounding, as opposed to starting in your 40s or 50s.

Contribute Regularly

Consistency is key. By making regular contributions to your investment accounts, you can take advantage of dollar-cost averaging, which can smooth out market volatility and optimize your returns over time. Whether it's monthly, quarterly, or annually, setting a routine helps ensure that your money is continually working to generate more wealth.

Reinvest Dividends

Instead of taking dividends as cash, reinvest them. Reinvesting dividends allows the earnings to compound further, accelerating the growth of your portfolio. Many brokerage services offer automatic reinvestment options, making it a hassle-free way to keep your investments growing.

Increase Contributions Over Time

Whenever possible, increase the amount you're contributing to your investments. Raises, bonuses, or any extra income can be funneled into your investment accounts. This not only boosts the principal amount but also amplifies the compounding effect.

Avoid Withdrawals

Resist the urge to dip into your investment accounts unless absolutely necessary. Withdrawals can significantly impede the growth potential of your portfolio, as it interrupts the compounding process. Letting your investments ride out market fluctuations and grow over time can yield far greater returns.

Diversify Smartly

Diversification can help manage risk while enabling growth. By spreading your investments across different asset classes such as stocks, bonds, mutual funds, and ETFs, you reduce the risk of loss while maximizing potential returns. Each asset class has its own compounding potential and together they create a more resilient portfolio.

Leverage Tax-Advantaged Accounts

Take full advantage of tax-deferred or tax-free growth opportunities available through various retirement accounts like 401(k)s and IRAs. These accounts allow your investments to grow without the drag of taxes, accelerating your compounding benefits.

Monitor and Rebalance

Regularly monitoring your portfolio and rebalancing as necessary ensures that your asset allocation remains aligned with your financial goals. Rebalancing can also capture gains and reinvest them, further maximizing the compounding effect.

Incorporating these strategies into your financial plan can significantly enhance the power of compound interest. By starting early, contributing consistently, reinvesting dividends, and smartly managing your portfolio, you set the stage for substantial wealth growth over time. Your commitment today can lead to a financially independent tomorrow.

Chapter 7: Retirement Accounts

You've come a long way in your journey to financial independence and wealth generation. Now, it's time to tackle one of the most vital aspects of any robust financial plan: retirement accounts. Understanding and maximizing these accounts can significantly impact your long-term financial health, ensuring that you not only survive but thrive in your golden years.

Introduction to 401k

A 401k is one of the most well-known retirement savings vehicles offered by employers. It's a powerful tool for accumulating wealth, primarily because it allows you to contribute pre-tax income, which can lower your taxable income for the year. Most employers also offer matching contributions, effectively giving you free money to boost your retirement savings.

Contributing to a 401k is straightforward. You decide how much of your paycheck you want to divert into the account, and the funds are automatically invested in the options your plan offers. These options often include various mutual funds, which spread your risk across a range of assets.

When investing in a 401k, consider the following steps:
1. Maximize your employer's match. Don't leave free money on the table.
2. Diversify your investments. Choose a mix of assets that aligns with your risk tolerance.
3. Regularly review and adjust your contributions and investments as needed.

Benefits of IRA

Individual Retirement Accounts (IRAs) offer another avenue for building retirement savings. Unlike 401ks, which are employer-sponsored, IRAs are set up individually. There are two main types: Traditional IRA and Roth IRA, each with its unique benefits.

Traditional IRAs allow you to contribute pre-tax income, which can lower your taxable income in the year you make the contribution. The earnings grow tax-deferred until you withdraw them in retirement. This can be particularly beneficial if you expect to be in a lower tax bracket during retirement.

Roth IRAs, on the other hand, involve contributions made with after-tax dollars. The significant advantage here is that both your contributions and earnings grow tax-free, and withdrawals in retirement are also tax-free, provided certain conditions are met.

Here are the key benefits of an IRA:
- **Tax-deferred growth:** With a Traditional IRA, you don't pay taxes on your earnings until you withdraw them.
- **Tax-free withdrawals:** Roth IRAs offer the benefit of tax-free withdrawals in retirement.
- **Flexibility:** You have a wide range of investment options, from stocks and bonds to mutual funds and ETFs.
- **Accessibility:** An IRA can be opened by anyone with earned income, providing a versatile option for various financial situations.

Roth vs Traditional IRA

Choosing between a Roth IRA and a Traditional IRA depends on your current financial situation and your expectations for the future. Let's break down the key differences to help you make an informed decision:

1. **Tax Treatment:** Traditional IRAs offer a tax break upfront, allowing you to defer taxes until you withdraw the money in retirement. In contrast, Roth IRAs involve paying taxes on your contributions now, but both the growth and withdrawals are tax-free.
2. **Income Limits:** Roth IRAs have income limits for contributions, which can phase out at higher income levels. Traditional IRAs don't have income limits for contributions, though the ability to deduct them may be affected by your income and participation in an employer-sponsored plan.
3. **Required Minimum Distributions (RMDs):** Traditional IRAs require you to start taking RMDs at age 72, while Roth IRAs do not have RMDs during your lifetime, offering greater flexibility in managing your retirement funds.

Consider these factors when deciding between a Roth and Traditional IRA. If you expect to be in a higher tax bracket during retirement, a Roth IRA might be more beneficial. If you prefer the tax break now and imagine a lower tax rate in retirement, a Traditional IRA could be the way to go.

Deciphering the complexities of retirement accounts can seem daunting, but it's an essential part of your path to financial independence. Every dollar you invest in these accounts today has the potential to grow exponentially, thanks to the power of compound interest, and provide you with the financial security and freedom you've always dreamed of.

In the next chapter, we'll explore the intriguing concept of Infinite Banking. Get ready to discover how you can become your own bank and harness your savings to generate even more wealth.

Introduction to 401k

When it comes to preparing for retirement, a 401k plan is often one of the most powerful tools at your disposal. Designed to help you save for your future, this type of retirement account offers several benefits that can be instrumental in achieving financial independence. So, let's dive in and discuss what a 401k is and why it's such a valuable asset for anyone looking to build their wealth and secure a comfortable retirement.

A 401k is a retirement savings plan sponsored by an employer. It allows employees to save and invest a portion of their paycheck before taxes are taken out. This means that you'll be able to grow your savings faster since contributions are made from your gross income, reducing your taxable income for the year. Most employers also offer some form of matching contribution, which is essentially free money added to your retirement savings.

One of the greatest advantages of a 401k plan is its potential for growth through investments. The money you contribute can be allocated into various investment options such as stocks, bonds, and mutual funds, enabling your savings to grow over time. The beauty of it lies in the power of compound interest, where your earnings generate earnings, creating a snowball effect that can significantly increase your nest egg by the time you retire.

Moreover, the contribution limits for 401k plans are quite generous. As of 2023, you can contribute up to \$22,500 annually, and if you're 50 or older, you're eligible for additional catch-up contributions, allowing you to save an extra \$7,500 per year. This feature is particularly helpful for those who start saving later in life and need to ramp up their retirement funds quickly.

While contributions to a traditional 401k are tax-deferred, meaning you won't pay taxes until you withdraw the money in retirement, there's also an option called the Roth 401k. Contributions to a Roth 401k are made with after-tax dollars, which means you've already paid taxes on the money you contribute, but qualified withdrawals in retirement are tax-free. Choosing between a traditional and Roth 401k depends on your current tax situation and future tax considerations, which will be discussed in further detail in later sections.

It's also essential to be aware of the rules regarding withdrawals. Generally, you can start withdrawing from your 401k without penalty after age 59½. If you take money out before this age, you might face a 10% early withdrawal penalty on top of regular income taxes, although there are some exceptions for specific circumstances.

In summary, a 401k is a key component of a well-rounded retirement strategy. It offers significant tax advantages, opportunities for employer matching contributions, and the potential for ample growth through compound interest. By maxing out your contributions and making informed investment choices, you can set yourself up for a financially secure and enjoyable retirement. Remember, the earlier you start, the more time your money has to grow, so consider taking full advantage of your 401k plan today.

Benefits of IRA

When planning for retirement, one crucial element to consider is an Individual Retirement Account (IRA). These accounts not only offer a practical means to save for the future but also come with a variety of benefits that can significantly enhance your financial situation.

Tax Advantages

One of the primary perks of contributing to an IRA is the tax advantages. With a Traditional IRA, your contributions might be tax-deductible, potentially lowering your taxable income for the year. In contrast, Roth IRA contributions are made with after-tax dollars, which means you won't get a tax break upfront, but your withdrawals in retirement are tax-free. Both options provide a strategic way to optimize your tax situation based on your current and expected future tax brackets.

Compound Interest

IRAs allow your money to grow exponentially through the magic of compound interest. The earlier you start and the more consistent you are with your contributions, the more you can benefit. Over time, your investment earnings start to generate their own earnings, creating a snowball effect that significantly boosts your retirement savings. This is an excellent way to make your money work for you while you're focusing on your career and other income streams.

Flexibility in Investment Choices

IRAs offer a broad range of investment options. Unlike 401(k) plans that often limit you to a predefined set of investments, IRAs allow you to invest in stocks, bonds, mutual funds, ETFs, and even real estate, depending on the provider. This flexibility enables you to tailor your investment strategy according to your risk tolerance, financial goals, and retirement timeline.

Access to Funds in Special Situations

While the goal is to let your contributions grow untouched until retirement, life's unpredictable nature sometimes necessitates early withdrawals. IRAs provide some leeway here. For instance, Roth IRAs allow for penalty-free withdrawals of your contributions (but not the earnings) at any time. Under specific circumstances like buying your first home or facing significant medical expenses, you might be able to withdraw from your Traditional IRA without incurring penalties. The rules can be intricate, but having these options can provide peace of mind.

Protection from Creditors

Another lesser-known benefit of IRAs is the creditor protection they offer. In many states, funds held within an IRA are protected from creditors' claims, even in the event of bankruptcy. This protection ensures that your retirement savings are safeguarded, offering you more security as you plan for the future.

In summary, IRAs are a powerful tool in your retirement planning arsenal. They offer significant tax benefits, the power of compound interest, flexible investment choices, and protections that other savings vehicles may not provide. Whether you choose a Traditional or Roth IRA, contributing to an IRA is a step toward financial independence and a secure retirement.

Roth vs Traditional IRA

When planning for retirement, choosing the right Individual Retirement Account (IRA) can make all the difference. Both Roth and Traditional IRAs offer unique advantages, but they cater to different financial strategies and goals. Understanding these differences can empower you to make informed decisions that align with your vision for financial independence.

Let's start with the basics. A Traditional IRA allows you to make contributions with pre-tax dollars, which can lower your taxable income for the year. In return, you'll pay taxes on the money when you withdraw it in retirement. This can be beneficial if you expect to be in a lower tax bracket when you retire. The immediate tax break provided by a Traditional IRA can be a big help in getting more funds invested sooner, potentially resulting in substantial growth over the years thanks to the power of compound interest.

On the other hand, contributions to a Roth IRA are made with after-tax dollars. This means you won't get a tax break upfront, but qualified withdrawals during retirement are tax-free. If you anticipate being in a higher tax bracket when you retire or prefer the certainty of tax-free income later in life, a Roth IRA might be a better fit for you. The ability to grow your investments tax-free can turn into significant savings over time, especially if you start contributing early and consistently.

Another key difference lies in the rules around withdrawals. Traditional IRAs require you to start taking Required Minimum Distributions (RMDs) at age 72. This means you're obligated to withdraw a certain amount each year, regardless of whether you need the money. These distributions will be taxed as ordinary income. On the flip side, Roth IRAs do not have RMDs during the account holder's lifetime. This can provide more flexibility in managing your retirement funds and potentially allow for greater wealth transfer to your heirs.

Considering income limits and contribution caps is also crucial. As of the latest tax guidelines, both Roth and Traditional IRAs have the same contribution limits, but eligibility for Roth IRA contributions does phase out at higher income levels. This means that if your income is above a certain threshold, you might not be able to contribute directly to a Roth IRA, although there are strategies like the "backdoor" Roth IRA conversion that can be used by higher-income earners.

So, which one should you choose? The answer often lies in your current tax situation, future income expectations, and retirement goals. If you're looking for an immediate tax break and believe you'll be in a lower tax bracket upon retirement, a Traditional IRA could be the way to go. If you're focused on long-term growth and tax-free withdrawals, a Roth IRA might be more suitable.

Ultimately, the choice between a Roth and Traditional IRA is a personal one, and it can even make sense to have both, balancing the benefits of tax-deferred and tax-free growth. Consulting with a financial advisor can provide personalized insights tailored to your unique financial landscape. By taking charge of your retirement planning now, you are setting the stage for a more financially secure and autonomous future.

Chapter 8: The Infinite Banking Concept

Imagine a financial strategy that lets you become your own bank. No, this isn't science fiction. It's called Infinite Banking, and it's a powerful way to take control of your finances. Infinite Banking allows you to leverage life insurance in a manner that's not commonly known or used. If you're tired of relying solely on traditional banking systems with their strict rules and limitations, this might just be the game-changer you've been waiting for.

What is Infinite Banking?

Simply put, Infinite Banking is a financial strategy that utilizes a specially-designed whole life insurance policy. This isn't your run-of-the-mill life insurance. Such policies are tailored for high cash value and low death benefit within the IRS regulations to maintain the tax benefits. The concept is based on the principles pioneered by Nelson Nash, who advocated for taking control of your own money through these meticulously crafted policies.

Here's the crux: You fund a whole life insurance policy, building its cash value over time. This cash value acts like a savings account but with benefits that are more far-reaching. You can borrow against this cash value at relatively low interest rates, essentially creating your personal bank where you're the lender and borrower. This bypasses traditional banking systems and their fees, loan schedules, and credit checks.

Implementing Infinite Banking

Let's delve into how you can put this transformative concept into action.

- **Step 1: Choose the Right Policy**

Start by consulting with a financial advisor who specializes in Infinite Banking. You'll need a whole life insurance policy designed to maximize cash value, not the generic type most insurance agents sell. This requires lower death benefits but higher contributions to the cash value.

- **Step 2: Fund Your Policy**

Once you've secured the right policy, you'll need to fund it consistently. This isn't much different from recurring investments. The key is to ensure that it's adequately funded so it builds significant cash value over time. The more you put in, the more you can leverage later on.

- **Step 3: Borrow and Repay**

When you need funds, borrow against your policy's cash value instead of going to a bank. The interest you pay goes back into your policy, effectively making you your own lender and borrower. This keeps the money within your financial ecosystem, working for you rather than a financial institution.

- **Step 4: Reinvest the Returns**

The cycle doesn't end with borrowing. The money you borrow can be used for various investments like real estate, stocks, or even starting a business. The returns from these investments can then be funneled back into your policy, enabling you to repeat the process with even more capital.

Many people using the Infinite Banking Concept find that it grants a level of financial flexibility and security that traditional methods can't match. You're not just creating wealth; you're also creating a self-sustaining financial system that grows with you.

So, are you ready to seize control of your financial future? With Infinite Banking, you're not just a player in the financial game; you're the banker, the investor, and the beneficiary all rolled into one. This could be the key to unlocking your path to true financial independence.

What is Infinite Banking?

Imagine a financial vehicle that allows you to take control of your own banking system, enabling you to borrow money and pay yourself back with interest, all while growing your wealth. Welcome to the concept of Infinite Banking. This isn't some modern-day invention or a fleeting trend; it's a long-standing financial strategy that taps into the power of whole life insurance policies.

At its core, Infinite Banking is about becoming your own banker. It revolves around using a specially designed whole life insurance policy to create a personal banking system. These policies are different from standard life insurance; they're structured to build cash value that grows tax-deferred over time. The magic lies in your ability to borrow against this cash value whenever you need to, whether it's for an emergency, an investment opportunity, or even to finance your next vehicle.

Why would you choose Infinite Banking over traditional banking? The reason is simple yet profound: control. Traditional banks operate with their own interests in mind, charging interest for the privilege of using their money. With Infinite Banking, you're recycling your own money and keeping the interest within your personal financial ecosystem. This accelerates wealth building, as the interest you'd typically pay to a bank gets paid to your policy, enhancing its growth.

One of the most compelling aspects of Infinite Banking is the uninterrupted compound interest. When you borrow against the cash value of your whole life policy, the remaining funds continue to grow as if you never touched them. This powerful feature means your money can work in two places simultaneously – financing your need and generating compound interest in your policy.

The Infinite Banking Concept is not just a strategy; it's a shift in how you view and manage your money. Implementing this approach requires a mindset that values financial independence and self-reliance. It involves diligent planning and disciplined execution, but the rewards are significant. You gain a lifetime financial tool that can serve as your personal bank, investment fund, and safety net, all rolled into one.

This concept isn't for everyone, and it's crucial to understand its intricacies fully before diving in. However, for those seeking a path to greater financial autonomy and wealth generation, Infinite Banking offers a compelling way forward. It's about taking control, leveraging your assets smartly, and creating a legacy of financial stability for yourself and your family.

In the following section, we'll delve into the specifics of how to implement Infinite Banking, exploring the steps needed to set up and manage your personal banking system effectively. But first, grasping the fundamental idea – the 'what' of Infinite Banking – sets the stage for the transformative journey towards financial empowerment.

Implementing Infinite Banking

So you've grasped the concept of Infinite Banking and are eager to put it into practice. How do you proceed from understanding theory to reaping the real-world benefits? Let's delve into the practical steps required to implement this powerful financial strategy.

First, it's essential to understand that Infinite Banking isn't a quick fix. It involves using a specially-designed whole life insurance policy as a tool to build and access your own cash flow. This isn't the typical life insurance policy you'd get for risk coverage; it needs to be specifically structured to maximize cash value growth.

The initial step is to find a knowledgeable advisor well-versed in Infinite Banking. An advisor skilled in this concept can design a policy tailored to your financial needs and goals. They will ensure the policy has the right blend of base premiums and paid-up additions to supercharge the cash value growth.

Next, fund your policy consistently. Just like any other investment, consistency is key. Regularly contributing to your policy not only builds the cash value faster but it also ensures you can leverage this value for loans and investments. Over time, you'll find that your policy's cash value becomes a significant source of liquidity.

One of the most compelling aspects of Infinite Banking is the loan feature. You can borrow against your policy's cash value for various purposes—whether it's investing in real estate, starting a business, or covering emergency expenses. The beauty here is that while you borrow from the policy, your cash value continues to grow tax-deferred, ensuring you don't miss out on compound interest.

These loans should be managed wisely. Keep in mind that even though you are borrowing from yourself, it's crucial to pay yourself back. Treat these loans with the same seriousness you'd treat a loan from a financial institution. This disciplined approach ensures that your policy's cash value remains robust and continues to grow year over year.

Moreover, the cash value in your policy becomes a financial buffer. This buffer can make all the difference during market downturns or personal financial hardships. When the traditional markets are volatile, having this cash reserve gives you peace of mind and financial stability.

Implementing Infinite Banking isn't just about managing cash flow; it's about fostering a mindset of financial independence. By controlling your banking function, you reduce dependency on traditional financial institutions and gain autonomy over your money. This independence is empowering, creating a foundation for long-term wealth generation.

Finally, continually educating yourself and adapting your strategy is essential. The financial landscape is ever-changing, and staying informed allows you to leverage your Infinite Banking strategy effectively. Attend workshops, read up on new financial tools, and never stop learning.

By taking these steps, you not only implement Infinite Banking but also set the stage for a more resilient and prosperous financial future. This strategy, when properly executed, can be a cornerstone in your journey towards achieving financial independence and building generational wealth.

Chapter 9: Real Estate Investments

Building wealth through real estate can be one of the most lucrative ways to achieve financial independence. Unlike other investment avenues, real estate has the unique benefit of providing both cash flow and appreciation. But diving into real estate can seem daunting, especially if you've never owned more than just your home. Let's walk through the basics to help you get started.

Introduction to Real Estate Investing

Firstly, it's essential to grasp why real estate is such a powerful investment tool. Real estate investing isn't just about buying properties; it's about generating passive income and building equity over time. When you invest in real estate, you're not just putting money into an asset; you're also buying an income stream that can last for years, even decades. Real estate investments typically fall into two main categories: residential and commercial properties. Each has its own set of opportunities and challenges, but both have the potential to build substantial wealth if managed wisely. Let's consider why real estate is a cornerstone for financial independence:

- **Cash Flow:** Rental properties can provide a steady monthly income, allowing you to cover expenses and potentially earn a profit. Over time, as rent prices increase, your cash flow improves.
- **Appreciation:** Property values tend to increase over the long term. While the market can fluctuate, real estate generally appreciates, helping you build equity in your investment.
- **Leverage:** Real estate allows you to use borrowed money to increase the potential return on investment. A relatively small down payment can control a much larger asset, multiplying the effects of your investment.
- **Tax Benefits:** There are numerous tax advantages to owning real estate, including depreciation, mortgage interest deductions, and other write-offs that can significantly reduce your taxable income.
- **Hedge Against Inflation:** Real estate values and rental income tend to rise with inflation, helping to protect your purchasing power over time.

Types of Real Estate Investments

Understanding the different types of real estate investments is crucial to making informed decisions. Each type has its own set of characteristics, risks, and rewards, so let's dive into the most common ones:

- **Residential Properties:** These include single-family homes, multifamily homes, condominiums, and townhouses. Investing in residential properties is a popular starting point due to their familiarity and relatively low barriers to entry.
- **Commercial Properties:** This category comprises office buildings, retail spaces, industrial properties, and more. Commercial real estate often requires a more significant investment but can provide higher returns and longer lease terms.
- **Rental Properties:** You can generate a steady income by owning rental properties. It requires managing tenants and maintaining the property, but it can be a reliable source of passive income.

- **Real Estate Investment Trusts (REITs):** For those who prefer not to manage properties directly, REITs offer a way to invest in real estate through the stock market. REITs are companies that own, operate, or finance income-generating real estate and pay out dividends to investors.
- **Vacation Rentals:** With the rise of platforms like Airbnb, investing in vacation rentals has become an attractive option. They can provide higher income per rental period but may require more management effort.
- **House Flipping:** This involves buying a property, renovating it, and selling it at a profit. It's a more hands-on approach that can yield significant returns but also comes with higher risks and a need for specialized knowledge.

Real estate investing is not a one-size-fits-all endeavor. Whether you prefer the hands-on approach of managing rental properties or the passive income from REITs, there's a strategy out there that fits your style and financial goals. The key is to start with clear objectives, perform thorough research, and be ready to adapt as you learn more. With careful planning and persistence, real estate can become a cornerstone of your wealth-building strategy.

Introduction to Real Estate Investing

Welcome to the exciting and rewarding world of real estate investing. This section marks the beginning of a journey that can lead you to financial independence and wealth generation. Real estate, with its tangible nature and potential for significant returns, has been a cornerstone of wealth for centuries. So, how can you tap into this lucrative market? Let's dive in.

First, it's essential to understand what real estate investing entails. At its core, it's about purchasing property as an investment to generate income rather than using it as a primary residence. This can be through rental income, future resale of the property, or a combination of both. The beauty of real estate lies in its versatility and the myriad of strategies available to investors.

One primary reason people are drawn to real estate is its potential for passive income. Imagine receiving monthly rental checks without having to clock into an office. It's a compelling prospect, isn't it? Rental properties can provide a steady stream of income that, over time, covers the property's costs and starts generating profit. The key here is due diligence—understanding the market, choosing the right property, and managing it efficiently.

Additionally, real estate can offer substantial tax benefits, making it an attractive option for those looking to optimize their financial portfolio. Deductions for mortgage interest, property depreciation, and various operating expenses can significantly impact your bottom line. To make the most of these benefits, it's advisable to work with a knowledgeable tax advisor who can guide you through the intricacies of real estate-related tax laws.

Another compelling factor is the appreciation potential. While the real estate market can fluctuate, properties generally tend to increase in value over the long term. This can lead to substantial capital gains upon selling the property. Think of it as planting a seed now that will grow into a significant financial asset in the years to come.

Real estate also offers a measure of control that's rare in other investment options. You're not just handing your money over and hoping for the best. Instead, you can take proactive steps to increase the property's value, such as making renovations, improving management practices, or finding better tenants. This hands-on approach can be incredibly satisfying and financially rewarding.

It's important, however, to acknowledge the challenges. Real estate investing requires significant upfront capital, and managing properties can be time-consuming. Market conditions can also impact returns. Therefore, education and preparation are crucial. Equip yourself with knowledge, build a solid network of professionals, and be prepared to navigate the ups and downs. With the right approach, the rewards can far outweigh the challenges.

In closing, real estate investing offers a path to financial independence that combines the stability of a tangible asset with opportunities for income, tax benefits, and appreciation. It's a field where strategy and savvy can yield significant returns. As we move forward, we'll explore the various types of real estate investments and delve deeper into how you can make the most of this powerful wealth generation tool.

Stay inspired and motivated, knowing that with knowledge and persistence, you can build a prosperous future through real estate investing.

Types of Real Estate Investments

Real estate investing is a versatile and potentially lucrative way to build your wealth. Understanding the different types of real estate investments can help you make informed decisions and tailor your strategy to fit your financial goals and risk tolerance. Let's dive into the various categories of real estate investments that you might consider.

- **Residential Properties:** These include single-family homes, multi-family residences, condominiums, townhouses, and vacation houses. Many investors start with residential real estate because it is straightforward to understand and can provide consistent rental income.
- **Commercial Properties:** This category encompasses office buildings, retail spaces, warehouses, and industrial properties. Commercial real estate typically involves longer lease agreements, which can provide a more stable income stream compared to residential properties.
- **Industrial Properties:** These properties are primarily used for manufacturing, storage, distribution, and research and development. Investing in industrial properties can yield high returns, especially in areas with significant industrial activity.
- **Retail Properties:** Retail real estate includes shopping centers, strip malls, and standalone stores. While retail investments can be profitable, they come with risks related to consumer trends and economic conditions.
- **Mixed-Use Properties:** These properties combine residential, commercial, and sometimes industrial spaces within a single project. Mixed-use developments can offer diversification and multiple streams of income from a single investment.
- **Real Estate Investment Trusts (REITs):** REITs allow you to invest in real estate without directly owning property. These companies own, operate, or finance income-generating real estate and distribute the bulk of their income to shareholders in the form of dividends. REITs offer liquidity and diversification, making them an appealing option for many investors.
- **Raw Land:** Investing in undeveloped land can be speculative but may offer substantial returns if the property appreciates over time or is developed. This type of investment requires careful research and consideration of factors like zoning laws, land use regulations, and future development plans.
- **Real Estate Crowdfunding:** With the rise of online platforms, investors can now participate in crowdfunding opportunities to invest in real estate projects. Crowdfunding allows you to pool your money with other investors to fund a project, typically at a lower entry cost compared to traditional real estate investments.

By diversifying across different types of real estate investments, you can balance risk and reward, achieving a more resilient and profitable portfolio. Keep in mind that each type of investment has its own nuances, requirements, and potential pitfalls. It's crucial to conduct thorough research and possibly consult with experts to ensure your investment aligns with your financial objectives.

Chapter 10: Tax Strategies for Wealth Generation

As we continue our journey toward financial independence, it's crucial to understand that taxes can significantly impact your ability to generate and retain wealth. Effective tax strategies are not just about saving money; they're about strategically planning your finances to ensure you keep more of what you earn. In this chapter, we'll explore some key tax strategies that can help you enhance your wealth generation efforts.

Understanding Tax Brackets

The first step in optimizing your tax strategy is understanding how tax brackets work. The U.S. tax system is progressive, which means the rate of taxation increases as your income increases. It's not just about the total income; it's more about how that income is divided across different brackets. Knowing your tax bracket can help you make informed decisions about income, deductions, and investments.

For instance, if you find yourself nearing the upper limit of a lower tax bracket, it might be beneficial to defer some income to the following year or accelerate deductions to remain in the lower bracket. This can potentially reduce your taxable income and the overall tax you need to pay.

Tax-Efficient Investing

Your investment strategy should also include tax considerations. Here are some tax-efficient investing tips:

1. **Utilize Tax-Advantaged Accounts:** Make the most of tax-advantaged accounts like 401(k)s, IRAs, and HSAs. Contributions to these accounts can reduce your taxable income, and the growth is tax-deferred or even tax-free in the case of Roth accounts.
2. **Capitalize on Capital Gains Rates:** Long-term capital gains tax rates are generally lower than ordinary income tax rates. Holding investments for more than a year can reduce your tax liability when you sell them.
3. **Tax-Loss Harvesting:** If you have investments that are currently in the red, consider selling them to realize a loss. These losses can offset gains you have realized elsewhere, reducing your taxable income.
4. **Dividend Income:** Opt for qualified dividends when possible, as they are taxed at a lower rate compared to ordinary income.

Strategic Charitable Donations

Donating to charities not only supports causes you care about but also comes with potential tax benefits. Consider strategies like:

- **Bunching Charitable Contributions:** Instead of donating a consistent amount every year, you can bunch multiple years of contributions into one year. This can help you exceed the standard deduction, allowing you to itemize and lower your taxable income.
- **Donating Appreciated Assets:** Instead of cash, donate appreciated stocks or other assets. This allows you to avoid capital gains taxes and still claim the full charitable deduction.

Tax Planning for Retirement

Effectively managing taxes doesn't end when you retire. Here are some strategies to consider:

1. **Roth Conversions:** Converting traditional IRA assets to a Roth IRA can be a strategic move. Although you'll pay taxes on the converted amount now, the funds grow tax-free and withdrawals are tax-free in retirement.
2. **Required Minimum Distributions (RMDs):** Starting at age 72, you're required to take minimum distributions from traditional retirement accounts. Failing to do so can result in hefty penalties. Plan ahead to manage these distributions tax-efficiently.
3. **Strategic Withdrawals:** Plan the order in which you draw down your retirement accounts to optimize tax impact. For instance, you might withdraw from taxable accounts first to let your tax-advantaged accounts continue growing.

Remember, the goal of these strategies isn't to avoid taxes, but to manage them in a way that maximizes your long-term wealth. Consulting with a qualified tax advisor can help tailor these strategies to fit your unique financial situation.

With a solid understanding of tax strategies under your belt, you're well on your way to making more informed financial decisions. In the next chapter, we'll delve into protecting your wealth through insurance—an often overlooked yet vital part of financial planning.

Understanding Tax Brackets

Grasping the concept of tax brackets is a fundamental step in any effective wealth generation strategy. The tax system might seem intricate, but once you break it down, it becomes much more manageable. Let's dive into how understanding tax brackets can empower you to make more informed financial decisions.

The U.S. tax system is progressive, which means that your income is taxed at different rates depending on how much you earn. These distinct income ranges are what we call tax brackets. Knowing your tax bracket can help you predict your tax liability and plan accordingly.

One essential point is that being in a higher tax bracket doesn't mean all your income is taxed at that higher rate. Instead, only the income that falls within a particular bracket gets taxed at the corresponding rate. Here's a simplified example to illustrate:

Imagine the tax brackets are as follows:
- 10% on income up to $10,000
- 12% on income from $10,001 to $40,000
- 22% on income from $40,001 to $85,000

If you earn $50,000, your taxes would look something like this:
1. $10,000 taxed at 10%
2. $30,000 ($40,000 - $10,000) taxed at 12%
3. $10,000 ($50,000 - $40,000) taxed at 22%

Understanding this structure allows you to see that not all your income is taxed at the highest rate you fall into. This awareness can help you make more precise financial decisions, especially when planning investments or additional income sources.

By strategically managing your income and deductions, you can minimize your tax liability and keep more of your money working for you. For instance, contributing to retirement accounts like a 401k or an IRA can reduce your taxable income, potentially bumping you down into a lower tax bracket. This means you pay less tax now while saving for your future, hitting two birds with one stone.

The key takeaway here is that tax brackets are not punitive, but opportunities to optimize your financial planning. When coupled with other tax-efficient strategies, a thorough understanding of your tax brackets can significantly contribute to your wealth-building journey.

Arming yourself with this knowledge is a motivational step towards achieving financial independence. As we move through this book, continue to reflect on how each piece of financial wisdom integrates with the broader picture of your wealth generation strategy. Remember, the better you understand the rules, the better you can play—and win—the game.

Tax-Efficient Investing

Tax-efficient investing is a cornerstone of building and maintaining wealth. It's not just about making money but keeping more of what you earn by strategically minimizing your tax burden. Let's dive into how you can achieve this through smart investment choices. First, it's essential to understand that not all investments are taxed equally. Some investments generate income that is taxed at a higher rate than others. Recognizing these differences can have a profound impact on your long-term wealth accumulation.

Tax-Advantaged Accounts

One of the simplest ways to invest tax-efficiently is by taking advantage of tax-advantaged accounts like 401(k)s and IRAs. Contributions to these accounts can lower your taxable income for the year, and the investments grow tax-deferred until withdrawal. When you eventually withdraw these funds, you'll likely be in a lower tax bracket, reducing the overall tax liability.

Capital Gains Considerations

Another key strategy is to focus on investments that generate long-term capital gains rather than short-term gains. Long-term capital gains are typically taxed at a lower rate than ordinary income. Holding investments for more than a year not only gives your money more time to grow but also ensures you benefit from these lower tax rates.

Dividend Stocks and Tax Efficiency

When it comes to dividend stocks, it's vital to distinguish between qualified and non-qualified dividends. Qualified dividends are taxed at the lower long-term capital gains rate, while non-qualified dividends are taxed at your ordinary income rate. Investing in companies that pay qualified dividends can be a tax-efficient way to generate income.

Municipal Bonds

Municipal bonds are another excellent tax-efficient investment. The interest earned from municipal bonds is generally exempt from federal income taxes. Depending on your state of residence, it might also be exempt from state and local taxes. While the returns might be lower compared to other bonds, the tax savings can make them a more attractive option for some investors.

Tax Loss Harvesting

Tax loss harvesting is a strategy that involves selling investments at a loss to offset gains in other areas of your portfolio. This can help reduce your taxable income for the year. While it might seem counterintuitive to sell at a loss, the tax benefits can be significant, making it a valuable tool in tax-efficient investing.

In conclusion, tax-efficient investing isn't about evading taxes but making informed decisions to minimize them legally. By understanding and utilizing tax-advantaged accounts, capital gains regulations, dividend taxation, municipal bonds, and tax loss harvesting, you can significantly enhance your wealth generation efforts. Your goal should be to grow and preserve your wealth strategically, ensuring you get to enjoy the fruits of your labor without excessive tax burdens.

Chapter 11: Protecting Your Wealth

So, you've worked hard to build your wealth. You've invested wisely, diversified your assets, and watched your financial goals come to fruition. But here's where many falter – they don't take steps to protect what they've earned. Protecting your wealth is just as important as accumulating it. Imagine building a sandcastle only to watch the tide wash it all away. That's what can happen if you don't shield your assets from potential threats.

Importance of Insurance

Insurance is fundamentally a safety net. It's there to catch you when something unexpected happens. From natural disasters to medical emergencies, life has a way of throwing curveballs. When such things happen, having the right insurance can mean the difference between a minor setback and a financial disaster.

There are several types of insurance to consider:

- **Health Insurance:** This is essential for covering medical expenses, which can otherwise deplete your savings quickly. A significant illness or accident without coverage can lead to astronomical bills.
- **Homeowner's or Renter's Insurance:** This protects against damage or loss of your home and personal property. Whether it's due to fire, theft, or other disasters, it ensures you're not left to start over from scratch.
- **Auto Insurance:** Required by law in most places, this covers damages incurred from accidents, theft, and other vehicle-related incidents.
- **Life Insurance:** This is crucial if you have dependents. It provides financial security for your loved ones if something happens to you.
- **Disability Insurance:** This covers a portion of your income if you become unable to work due to a disability, ensuring you can still meet your financial obligations.
- **Long-Term Care Insurance:** As we age, the odds of needing long-term care increase. This insurance helps cover the costs of care that aren't typically covered by health insurance, Medicare, or Medicaid.

Types of Insurance

Choosing the right insurance policy often involves a balance between coverage and premiums. Let's break down some common types:

- **Term Life Insurance:** Offers coverage for a specific period. It's generally less expensive and is ideal for those who need coverage for a confined time, such as until children are grown or a mortgage is paid off.
- **Whole Life Insurance:** Provides lifetime coverage and includes an investment component known as the policy's cash value.
- **Universal Life Insurance:** This offers flexibility in premiums and death benefits. It also includes a savings element that grows on a tax-deferred basis.
- **Umbrella Insurance:** This provides additional liability coverage beyond other insurance policies, protecting your savings and other assets if you're sued.
- **Critical Illness Insurance:** Provides a lump sum cash payment if you're diagnosed with a specified illness, such as cancer or heart disease.

It's not just about having insurance; it's about having the right insurance. Review your policies regularly to ensure they meet your current needs.

Additionally, consider legal avenues like trusts and wills. Drafting a robust estate plan ensures your wealth is distributed according to your wishes and minimizes the tax burden on your heirs. Trusts can protect your assets from creditors and legal disputes.

Remember, protecting your wealth isn't just about holding onto what you have. It's about creating a resilient financial foundation that can weather any storm. Insurance and estate planning are pillars of that foundation. By safeguarding your assets, you ensure that the wealth you've worked so hard to build remains intact, providing security and peace of mind for you and your loved ones.

Importance of Insurance

When it comes to protecting your wealth, there's one tool that's often overlooked but incredibly vital: insurance. Think of insurance as the safety net that catches you when life throws its curveballs. Whether it's a sudden health issue, an unexpected loss, or even natural disasters, insurance serves as your financial armor, shielding your hard-earned assets and ensuring that a single unfortunate event doesn't derail all your efforts towards financial independence.

Insurance essentially buys you peace of mind. Knowing that you have a reliable backup plan in place allows you to focus more on wealth creation and less on what might go wrong. While it's natural to prioritize investments, saving, and income generation, the importance of a solid insurance plan can't be overstated. It acts as a cornerstone of a well-rounded financial strategy, providing a blend of protection and growth opportunities.

Diverse types of insurance can cover a wide range of potential risks. Health insurance can prevent medical bills from draining your savings. Life insurance ensures your loved ones are taken care of if something happens to you. Home and auto insurance protect your physical assets. Disability insurance safeguards your income stream in case you're unable to work. Simply put, the right insurance policies can do more than just protect you—they can uphold the financial stability you've worked so hard to build.

Moreover, having proper insurance in place can contribute to your overall wealth-building strategy. Some insurance plans come with investment components that can yield returns, offering a dual benefit of protection and growth. These plans can align well with your long-term financial goals, providing an additional avenue for wealth generation while ensuring you are covered against potential setbacks.

Weave insurance into your financial planning as diligently as you do with budgeting or investing. Consult experts to determine what types of insurance you need and adjust as your financial situation evolves. It's not just about checking off a box; it's about strategically protecting and enhancing your wealth. The goal here is to create a resilient financial fortress, and insurance is an indispensable part of that fortress.

In summary, insurance is a key component of wealth protection. It offers critical coverage for various risks, providing both security and opportunities for growth. By incorporating insurance into your financial strategy, you're not just safeguarding your present—you're fortifying your future.

Types of Insurance

Insurance isn't just a safety net; it's an essential cornerstone for protecting your wealth. While we work hard to build our assets and safeguard our future, it's critical to understand the various types of insurance that can help mitigate risks and prevent financial losses. Each type of insurance serves a distinct purpose, ensuring that you're covered from multiple angles.

1. Health Insurance
Health insurance is a must-have. Medical emergencies can strike without warning, and the financial impact can be devastating. A good health insurance plan covers hospital stays, surgeries, prescription drugs, and sometimes even preventive care, ensuring that your savings and investments aren't wiped out by unexpected medical bills.

2. Life Insurance
Life insurance provides financial security for your loved ones in the event of your untimely death. It helps cover funeral costs, outstanding debts, and can even replace lost income, allowing your family to maintain their standard of living. There are different types of life insurance, such as term life and whole life, each with its own set of benefits and considerations.

3. Disability Insurance
Disability insurance protects your income if you become unable to work due to illness or injury. Short-term and long-term policies are available, offering various levels of coverage. This insurance ensures that a temporary or permanent disability won't hinder your financial goals.

4. Homeowners Insurance
Your home is likely one of your most significant investments. Homeowners insurance covers damage to your home and its contents from events like fires, theft, and natural disasters. Additionally, it provides liability coverage in case someone gets injured on your property.

5. Auto Insurance
Auto insurance is not only legally required but also essential for protecting your vehicle investment. It covers damages from accidents, theft, and other incidents. Liability coverage also protects you from financial ruin if you're found responsible for causing injury or property damage to others.

6. Umbrella Insurance
Umbrella insurance offers additional liability coverage that goes beyond the limits of your homeowners, auto, or boat insurance policies. It provides an extra layer of security, especially if you have significant assets that could be targeted in a lawsuit.

7. Long-Term Care Insurance
As we age, the need for long-term care might become a reality. Long-term care insurance helps cover the costs of assisted living, nursing homes, and home health care. This can be crucial in preserving your retirement funds and other savings for their intended purposes.

- Health Insurance
- Life Insurance
- Disability Insurance
- Homeowners Insurance

- Auto Insurance
- Umbrella Insurance
- Long-Term Care Insurance

By understanding and investing in the right types of insurance, you're taking a significant step towards protecting your wealth. The peace of mind that comes with being well-insured can't be underestimated, offering you the security to pursue your financial goals with confidence.

Chapter 12: Creating a Financial Independence Plan

Financial independence isn't just a distant dream—it's a tangible goal you can achieve with careful planning and disciplined execution. Creating a financial independence plan is a vital step in your journey towards freedom. This chapter focuses on actionable steps and strategies to help you forge a clear, effective plan to secure your financial future.

Steps to Create Your Plan

Here are some essential steps to guide you in crafting a robust financial independence plan:

1. **Assess Your Current Financial Situation:** The first step is to take a close look at where you stand financially. Evaluate your income, expenses, debts, and savings. This will give you a clear picture of your starting point.
2. **Set Clear and Achievable Goals:** Define what financial independence means to you. Whether it's retiring early, traveling the world, or starting a new venture, your goals should be specific, measurable, attainable, relevant, and time-bound (SMART).
3. **Create a Detailed Budget:** A well-constructed budget is the foundation of any financial plan. Categorize your expenses and prioritize needs over wants. Look for opportunities to cut unnecessary spending and increase your saving rate.
4. **Establish Multiple Income Streams:** Relying on a single source of income can be risky. Explore additional income avenues such as side businesses, freelance work, or investments that generate passive income.
5. **Invest Wisely:** Investing is a powerful tool to grow your wealth. Diversify your portfolio to balance risk and reward. Understand different investment vehicles like stocks, bonds, real estate, and how they fit into your overall strategy.
6. **Build an Emergency Fund:** Life is unpredictable, and having an emergency fund can protect you from unforeseen financial shocks. Aim to save at least three to six months' worth of living expenses.
7. **Plan for Tax Efficiency:** Understand your tax obligations and look for ways to minimize your tax liability legally. Utilize tax-advantaged accounts and consider consulting with a tax professional.
8. **Regularly Review and Adjust Your Plan:** A strong financial plan isn't set in stone. Circumstances change, and your plan should be flexible enough to adapt. Review your progress at least annually and make adjustments as needed.

Adjusting Your Plan Over Time

Creating a financial independence plan isn't a one-time task; it's an ongoing process that requires regular adjustments. Here's how you can keep your plan dynamic and responsive to changes:

- **Stay Informed:** Keep yourself updated with financial news, market trends, and changes in tax laws. The more informed you are, the better decisions you'll make.

- **Monitor Your Progress:** Track your financial milestones and celebrate small victories along the way. Use tools and apps to help you stay organized and on top of your goals.
- **Reevaluate Your Goals:** As you grow and your circumstances evolve, so might your goals. Periodically reassess what financial independence means to you and adjust your plan accordingly.
- **Seek Professional Advice:** Don't hesitate to consult financial advisors or planners. They can provide valuable insights and help you navigate complex financial situations.
- **Stay Disciplined:** Consistency is key. Stick to your budget, follow your investment plan, and resist the temptation to make impulsive financial decisions.

Remember, creating and maintaining a financial independence plan is a journey, not a destination. By staying focused, disciplined, and adaptable, you can build a secure financial future that allows you to live life on your own terms.

Steps to Create Your Plan

Creating a financial independence plan requires a clear and structured approach. It's not about hoping for the best, but laying down a concrete roadmap that will take you from where you are today to where you want to be. Let's break down the key steps you'll need to take to craft a plan that works for you.

1. **Assess Your Current Financial Situation:** Start by taking a thorough look at your current finances. This means listing out all your assets, liabilities, income, and expenses. Know your net worth and understand where your money is coming from and where it's going. This honest assessment sets the foundation for your financial plan.

1. **Set Clear Financial Goals:** Identify what financial independence means to you. Is it retiring at a certain age? Living off passive income? Traveling the world? Break these goals down into short-term, medium-term, and long-term milestones. Prioritize them based on what's most important to you.

1. **Create a Realistic Budget:** With your goals in mind, craft a budget that reflects your financial realities and aspirations. Ensure you allocate funds towards savings and investments while managing your daily expenses. A budget isn't about restricting your life; it's about making informed choices that align with your goals.

1. **Establish Multiple Income Streams:** Relying on a single source of income can be risky. Explore opportunities like passive income, real estate investments, and dividend stocks. Diversifying your income streams can provide financial stability and accelerate your path to independence.

1. **Invest Wisely:** Educate yourself about the various investment options available. Whether it's stocks, bonds, mutual funds, or ETFs, make informed decisions based on your risk tolerance and timeframe. Compounding interest is powerful; the earlier you start, the more your investments will grow.

1. **Plan for Retirement:** Understand the different types of retirement accounts such as 401(k)s, IRAs, and Roth IRAs. Utilize these accounts to maximize your savings and benefit from tax advantages. Planning for retirement is crucial to financial independence.

1. **Implement Tax Strategies:** Be proactive about tax planning. Familiarize yourself with tax brackets and explore tax-efficient investing strategies. Minimizing your tax liabilities can significantly boost your savings and investments over time.

1. **Protect Your Wealth:** Insurance plays a critical role in safeguarding your financial future. Health, life, and property insurance can protect you from unforeseen setbacks. Ensure you have the right coverage to mitigate risks.

1. **Monitor and Adjust Your Plan:** Financial planning isn't set in stone. Regularly review your progress and make adjustments as needed. Life circumstances change, and your plan should be flexible enough to adapt.
2. **Stay Educated:** Financial independence requires continuous learning. Stay updated with financial news, read books, and consider seeking advice from financial advisers. The more knowledgeable you are, the better decisions you can make.

These steps form a comprehensive approach to achieving financial independence. By taking deliberate actions and staying committed to your plan, you're on the path to generating wealth and gaining financial freedom. Remember, the journey may be long, but each step you take brings you closer to your ultimate goal.

Adjusting Your Plan Over Time

Achieving financial independence isn't a set-it-and-forget-it journey. You need to constantly evaluate and tweak your plan to stay on course. Life is full of changes—some expected, some not. Job changes, market fluctuations, health issues, and unexpected expenses can all impact your financial trajectory. That's why it's crucial to build flexibility into your financial independence plan and be prepared to make adjustments.

Regularly Reviewing Your Goals

Your financial goals aren't set in stone. What you aspire to at age 35 might look very different at age 50. Regularly review your short-term and long-term goals to ensure they still align with your life aspirations. It's recommended to revisit these goals at least once a year and make adjustments as necessary. If you've reached a significant milestone, don't hesitate to set new, more ambitious targets. This keeps you motivated and disciplined.

Tracking Your Progress

You can't manage what you don't measure. Keep track of your income, expenses, savings, and investments. Use tools like spreadsheets or financial management apps to monitor your progress. Regular tracking helps you spot trends and identify areas where you might need to cut back or adjust. It also provides the satisfaction of seeing your progress, which reinforces positive behavior and keeps you motivated.

Rebalancing Your Investments

Over time, the value of your investments will change. This can lead to a portfolio that's too risky or too conservative based on your current goals and risk tolerance. Regular rebalancing ensures that your investments remain aligned with your risk profile. Typically, you should review your portfolio at least once a year and make necessary adjustments. This can involve selling assets that have performed well and buying more of those that haven't, keeping your portfolio balanced.

Updating Your Budget

Your budget is a living document. As your income increases or decreases, or as your expenses shift, make sure to update your budget accordingly. Adding a new income stream or cutting down on unnecessary expenses can dramatically alter your financial outlook. Consistently updating your budget helps you stay disciplined and focused on your financial goals.

Adapting to Life Changes

Life is unpredictable. Whether it's a new job, a new family member, or an unforeseen expense, your financial plan needs to adapt. Be prepared to pivot and adjust your financial strategies as your life circumstances change. Having an emergency fund can provide a buffer, allowing you to adapt to changes without completely overhauling your financial plan.

Seeking Professional Advice

Don't hesitate to consult with a financial advisor to get a fresh perspective on your plan. Professional advice can offer insights you might not have considered and can help you navigate complex financial landscapes. A good advisor can help you identify potential adjustments and ensure you're on track to meet your goals.

Adjusting your plan over time isn't just about making changes when things go wrong; it's about being proactive and optimizing your strategy to maximize your wealth-generating potential. Stay flexible, stay informed, and most importantly, stay committed to your journey towards financial independence.

Conclusion

We've covered a lot of ground together, from the basics of financial independence to detailed strategies for investing, saving, and protecting your wealth. The journey to financial independence isn't just about accumulating money; it's about building a life where you have the freedom to make choices that align with your values and dreams.

Remember, every small step you take today can lead to significant gains tomorrow. By setting clear financial goals, creating a robust budget, and exploring multiple income streams, you're laying down the building blocks for your financial future. The power of compound interest and strategic investments can exponentially grow your wealth over time, allowing you to enjoy the fruits of your labor.

Utilize the knowledge of retirement accounts and tax strategies to maximize your savings and protect what you've earned through insurance and thoughtful planning. Each chapter in this book has provided you with tools and insights to create a personalized plan for achieving financial independence.

The key to success is consistency and adaptability. Regularly review your plan, adjust as life changes, and stay committed to your financial goals. Wealth generation is a dynamic process that requires persistence and continuous learning. Embrace the journey with a positive mindset and a willingness to adapt and grow.

Your financial independence is within reach. With determination, informed decisions, and a proactive approach, you can create a secure and prosperous future. Here's to your journey toward financial freedom and the abundant, fulfilling life that awaits you!

Appendix A: Appendix

As we wrap up this guide to achieving financial independence and generating wealth, it's crucial to arm yourself with additional resources and insights. Building a robust financial knowledge base will help you make informed decisions and stay ahead of the game. This appendix provides curated resources and recommended reading to further your journey toward financial freedom. Let's dive in.

Financial Independence Resources

There are numerous tools and resources available to help you navigate the path to financial independence. Here's a list of some valuable ones:

- **Personal Finance Software:** *Mint, YNAB (You Need A Budget), and Quicken* are excellent for tracking expenses, setting budgets, and managing investments.
- **Investment Platforms:** *Vanguard, Fidelity, and Charles Schwab* offer low-cost investment options and valuable educational resources for both beginners and seasoned investors.
- **Retirement Planning Resources:** Websites like *401k.org* and *RothIRA.com* provide comprehensive information on different retirement accounts and strategies to maximize your retirement savings.
- **Online Financial Communities:** Platforms such as *Bogleheads, Reddit's r/financialindependence, and Mr. Money Mustache Forums* are great for crowd-sourced advice and support from like-minded individuals and experts.

Recommended Reading

The following books and authors have been influential in the field of personal finance and wealth generation. Each offers unique perspectives and strategies to help you on your path:

1. *Your Money or Your Life* by Joe Dominguez and Vicki Robin - A classic that explores the relationship between time and money, helping you understand the value of financial independence.
2. *The Total Money Makeover* by Dave Ramsey - Provides a straightforward approach to debt reduction, budgeting, and wealth building.
3. *Rich Dad Poor Dad* by Robert T. Kiyosaki - Offers a different take on money and investing, urging readers to think outside the traditional education and employment paradigms.
4. *The Millionaire Next Door* by Thomas J. Stanley and William D. Danko - Examines the habits and behaviors of America's wealthy, revealing that financial success often comes from living below your means.
5. *I Will Teach You to Be Rich* by Ramit Sethi - Combines practical advice with a no-nonsense attitude, focusing on automating finances and smart investing.

These resources and books serve as powerful tools to expand your financial knowledge. Remember, the journey to financial independence is ongoing. Continually educating yourself, adapting strategies, and seeking new insights will be key to your success.

Here's to your prosperous future and the wealth you seek to build. Stay informed, stay motivated, and stay committed to your financial goals. The road to financial independence may require effort and persistence, but the rewards are undeniably worth it.

Financial Independence Resources

Finding the right resources can make all the difference when you're on the journey to financial independence. Below is a carefully curated list of tools, websites, and services that can help you stay on track and achieve your wealth generation goals.

- **Personal Finance Websites:** These can offer invaluable advice, calculators, and tools for budgeting, investing, and planning. Examples include sites like *Bankrate*, *Investopedia*, and *NerdWallet*.
- **Financial Planning Software:** Tools such as *Mint*, *YNAB (You Need A Budget)*, and *Personal Capital* are excellent for keeping track of your income, expenses, and investments. They can help you set and maintain your financial goals.
- **Budgeting Apps:** Apps like *Goodbudget*, *PocketGuard*, and *Wally* can help you manage your budget on the go.
- **Investment Platforms:** Platforms such as *Robinhood*, *E*TRADE*, and *Betterment* offer user-friendly ways to start investing in stocks, ETFs, and other securities.
- **Retirement Planning Resources:** Websites like *Fidelity*, *Vanguard*, and *Charles Schwab* provide tools and calculators to help you plan for retirement, including 401(k) and IRA options.
- **Books on Financial Independence:** Expand your knowledge with recommended readings such as *Your Money or Your Life* by Joe Dominguez and Vicki Robin, *The Millionaire Next Door* by Thomas J. Stanley and William D. Danko, and *Rich Dad Poor Dad* by Robert T. Kiyosaki.
- **Podcasts and Blogs:** Stay updated with the latest tips and strategies by tuning in to podcasts like *ChooseFI* and reading blogs such as *Mr. Money Mustache* and *The Simple Dollar*.
- **Financial Advisors:** Sometimes you need personalized advice. Consider consulting certified financial planners or advisors who can guide you tailored to your specific situation.

Leveraging these resources will provide you with the knowledge and tools you need to succeed on your path to financial independence. Remember, the key is to stay informed and use these tools to make educated financial decisions. Happy wealth-building!

Recommended Reading

Embarking on the journey to financial independence and wealth generation is a continuous learning process. To sustain your momentum and deepen your understanding, a curated list of valuable books is essential. Below, you'll find a selection of highly recommended reads that complement the strategies and principles discussed in this book. These resources will not only provide additional insights but also offer diverse perspectives on achieving financial success.

- **"Rich Dad Poor Dad" by Robert T. Kiyosaki:** An essential read that contrasts different attitudes towards money and investing, illustrating how mindset can shape your financial destiny.
- **"The Total Money Makeover" by Dave Ramsey:** A step-by-step guide to transforming your financial habits. Ramsey's no-nonsense approach to budgeting and debt reduction is motivating and actionable.
- **"The Intelligent Investor" by Benjamin Graham:** A classic in the world of investing. Graham's principles of value investing are timeless and provide a solid foundation for making informed investment decisions.
- **"Your Money or Your Life" by Vicki Robin and Joe Dominguez:** This book redefines the relationship between time and money, encouraging readers to align their spending with their values and achieve financial independence.
- **"Unshakeable" by Tony Robbins:** An excellent primer on investing, particularly for those who may be new to the subject. Robbins breaks down complex financial concepts into manageable, practical advice.
- **"The Millionaire Next Door" by Thomas J. Stanley and William D. Danko:** An insightful look at the habits and characteristics of America's wealthy, emphasizing the importance of frugality, discipline, and wise investments.
- **"Think and Grow Rich" by Napoleon Hill:** While not exclusively about financial advice, Hill's exploration of the power of mindset and perseverance is crucial for anyone aiming to build wealth.
- **"The Simple Path to Wealth" by JL Collins:** Focused on stock market investing with a minimalist approach. Collins simplifies investment strategies, making financial independence accessible.

Each of these books has been selected for its ability to provide profound insights, practical advice, and inspiration. They cover a broad spectrum of fiscal philosophies and strategies, reflecting the multifaceted nature of financial independence. Whether you're just starting or looking to refine your current approach, these reads will serve as valuable companions on your journey to wealth generation.

As you continue to educate yourself, remember that knowledge itself is a form of wealth. The more you learn, the better equipped you'll be to make informed decisions that will shape your financial future for the better.

www.ingramcontent.com/pod-product-compliance
Lightning Source LLC
Chambersburg PA
CBHW072053230526
45479CB00010B/948